# Alcohol Companion
## By Phil Cain

D0528080

First Edition (Refreshed February 2018)

ISBN-13: 978-1533234230
ISBN-10: 153323423X

To my companions.

# Contents

Introduction.................................................9

Stubborn elixir.............................................22

Of mice and men.........................................37

Great expectations.......................................40

Neural Trojan..............................................55

First contact ...............................................76

Bottled desire..............................................86

In the moment ............................................95

Groupdrink ...............................................111

And so to bed.............................................116

The morning after ........................................124

Downing drinks ........................................136

A diffuse affliction ........................................144

Blurred labyrinth ........................................151

Processor jamming ........................................161

Where there's a will ........................................171

Wilfully ill? ........................................185

Splitting the spectrum ........................................189

The pursuit of happiness ........................................206

Index ........................................213

# Acknowledgements

This book would not exist were it not for the dedicated work of thousands of alcohol research scientists over many years. In drawing together these findings, I relied on the help of the US National Institute on Alcohol Abuse and Alcoholism, the European Alcohol Policy Alliance, Alcohol Research UK and the charity Alcohol Concern. I also depended on the Karl Franzens University library in Graz, Austria to gain access to research material. And, last but not least, the enterprise would not have been possible without the cheerful support of my friends, colleagues and readers of the *philcain.com* blog.

Thank you. ∎

# Introduction

Thankfully alcohol is not a life-and-death issue for most of us, but it can still have a significant impact. Around 2 billion of us consume alcohol each year.[1] Yet few of us have a clear idea of why we drink or what effects it has. It might help to change that. Science has limitations here, as in any field, but it also offers some potentially useful insights.

We tend to muddle along, not giving it much thought. It is woven so deeply into our lives it can seem we are inseparable. We are born with alcohol-friendly architecture in our brains which means we find it hard not to think of it affectionately. It has carved out special places in our homes and refrigerators. Alcohol slips into our lives with such satisfying ease it seems foolish to complicate it. But, to understand it, we must.

We are often too close to alcohol to get a clear view of it. Like a faith or a friend, it offers us a source of comfort and feelings of safety and wellbeing. It can become a touchstone for us, offering a reliable resource in good times and bad. But even our deepest affections can sometimes be misplaced, sometimes attaching us to untrustworthy partners or dangerous toys. We are naturally prone to develop fond feelings for a drug of dependency.

Like animals right up the evolutionary chain, from fruit flies up to rats, mice, elephants and monkeys, we respond favourably to alcohol. But this hardwired appreciation does not mean it is an essential part of our lives or our societies. That is history, the past. We have used our extraordinary powers of invention to make our innate tolerance and appreciation of alcohol into more than the evolutionary accident it is. It is a construction we can, in theory, examine, disassemble and change as we prefer.

We can set aside familiar explanations when it serves our long-term needs. Our ancestors saw the sun move across the sky for millions of years and span a million satisfying fables to explain it, none of them a reliable description. But we did eventually manage to reject the emotionally engaging tales handed down to us and embraced the peculiar truth, accepting strange and implausible distances and masses, and ideas like gravitation, quantum mechanics. And there can be few clearer everyday examples of an area where systematic thought might help us. We could potentially save ourselves enormous discomfort and confusion.

But few outside research circles are familiar with more than a few scraps of research which make it into newspapers. These scraps add up to a curious collection. Any attempt to talk about the subject in a more comprehensive and balanced way is liable to be dismissed as the rhetoric of a "nannying elite" which, for reasons unknown, is bent on spoiling our fun.

So, our approach to alcohol is not generally greatly troubled by science, typically guided by a hot-potch of ideas picked up as we go through life, a concoction of odds and ends we comfortingly call "common sense". We like to think of common sense as a body of ideas patiently tweaked to near-perfection over the generations, with us adding our own certain something at the end. In reality, however, it is a strange body of often-contradictory and misguided folklore which helps muddle our beliefs and misguide our behaviour.

We should ignore common sense. Going along with its vagaries means our alcohol drinking can more easily become erratic and excessive, causing us problems. In our twenties many of us veer into alcohol dependence, where our brains adapt to alcohol, only to become more abstemious as we face the demands of jobs and families. Some carry on as we did in our twenties, however, or shift back and forth. At any one time, around one-in-ten men in the English-speaking world is alcohol dependent, meaning their brains have adapted to long-term alcohol exposure, and about half that proportion of women.[2]

Few of us know where we are on the spectrum of drinking, how we got there, or what it might mean? How can we be expected to manage the situation? Finding a more consistent foundation for ourselves could help make us safer and happier. As in other areas of life, a more accurate picture should help expand our choices and reduce the risk we face. A sailor would be foolish to ignore the weather forecast before casting off, as would a musician who began composing songs without some rudimentary idea of chord theory. Why should alcohol be any different?

There is nothing to lose from knowledge, although it may seem to threaten the "magic" of alcohol. Basic physics does not put illusionists out of business, but it saves us from being swindled. We can enjoy conjuring tricks for what they are. Does a god row a fiery celestial orb across the sky each day or do we live on a rock whizzing around a giant nuclear fusion reaction? Nothing in the immediate world around us changes from a more accurate understanding, but we have a better foundation for our thoughts and feelings. We are also better able to predict what will happen next and what will not. This is true for alcohol too.

Replacing our malleable common sense ideas about alcohol with something more rigid is no easy task, however. The breadth and complexity of alcohol's effects do not allow for swift and easy explanation. To get anywhere, we need to make what seem like sizable diversions to establish some groundwork and to sweep up the phenomena it leaves behind. This is why this is a book rather than an article. Its goal is descriptive, but it will offer a few ideas and observations to help tie it together.

It tracks the phases of a typical life of drinking, from our first contact with alcohol to recovery from dependence. In going between these two distant points, it stops to look at: happiness; our misguided attempt to make alcohol a medicine; neuroscience; the limits of scientific enquiry; the role of our beliefs in behaviour; and how alcohol fits into ideas of free will and our ability to control our destiny.

To make the practical advice plain from the start, we should not drink too much alcohol, if any. We can find the latest daily and weekly guideline maximums quite easily. They are no guarantee of trouble-free drinking, but they make the risk low. This book has no business second-guessing official guidance. But useful as they are, knowing where we want to finish is not the problem. The difficulty is in getting there.

The field of alcohol research is broad and does not give up its secrets lightly. Progress has been incremental, delivering results which can almost always be contested. A shift in understanding can often come through hair-splitting about statistical results rather than in some eureka moment. We can also sometimes find a metaphor can be a breakthrough, helpfully parcelling together disparate ideas. Distinctions too can help by cleaving apart common-sense ideas into their independent components.

The underlying reason for all this difficulty is that alcohol's main impact is on the brain, which nobody understands. It is more bewildering than the workings of the financial markets, economy, or weather. It is a web of billions of exquisitely delicate, interconnected components not understood even in isolation. Alcohol's warping effects only multiply the difficulty.

Our brains are not all the same either, meaning our responses to alcohol can be dramatically different, differences added to by variations in our digestion of alcohol. We also respond differently at different times depending on our surroundings and psychological state and past exposure. And our response also depends on our expectations, beliefs which vary between us and change.

Appreciating the impossibility of obtaining a complete answer to the problem should not stop us appreciating the value of a mosaic of answers. It is a significant improvement on the shifting sands of common sense which frequently misleads. Understanding alcohol's effects better at a scientific level can help us make better decisions, improving our well-being.

The science is not enough on its own though. We also need to identify and dismantle the thoughts, feelings and associations we already have. We have a relationship with alcohol, like one with a living person, or at least like one we might have with an old car.

This relationship starts to develop even before we come into direct contact with alcohol. As children, we start to form our first impressions of alcohol by watching other people drink it. It is the stuff of the imagination. Over our lifetimes, we consume many more imaginary alcoholic drinks than we ever have real ones. To these imaginings, we add anecdotes and impressions from the media, which we top up with our own experiences. These all accumulate into a kind of clay we can mould to explain our behaviour and that of others. The conclusions we sculpt from it tend to back up what we are doing; the more alcohol we are drinking, the more highly we tend to regard alcohol drinking, and vice versa. We are like politicians, skilfully shaping a satisfying story to fit the facts on the ground. Consistency and facts matter less than how it plays in our heads.

We commonly link alcohol with happiness and success, for example, a link the alcohol industry is only too happy to reinforce. There are, however, far stronger statistical links between alcohol and gloom and mistakes. We also often link alcohol to freedom, though it diminishes the mental resources we use to assert our autonomy. We "drink to forget" while alcohol preserves old memories and stops us gathering fresh ones. As rebellious teenagers, we are typically unaware our enthusiasm for alcohol tends to ape that of our parents.

We behave drunkenly when given placebo drinks. And some of us can even start to behave half-cut when we only hear some drink-related words. Properly inebriated we can have false beliefs too. We tend to feel more confident and relaxed, while our cognitive and physical abilities are blunted.

The pros and cons of alcohol have, of course, been argued about for as long as it has been around, which is a long time. The two main positions seem unlikely to have changed over the millennia. Alcohol is either a bad thing, full-stop, or, as Shakespeare's scheming Iago puts it in Othello, "a good familiar creature, if it be well used".[3] In modern terms, alcohol is positive, and all problems are the consumer's fault.

The alcohol industry has taken Iago's position and run with it. Its "responsible drinking" programmes are the work of marketing genius, allowing it to blame the customer for all the problems with its product, while also pushing their alcohol brands. "Why not have a nice ice-cold beer?" they say, "Just mind you do not drink too much." Life is richly rewarding for a fox trusted with a hen house.

We can read about a misty glen and babbling burn on the side of a whisky bottle, or the pastoral bliss in which a wine was produced, without a mention of the effects of the contents. These effects are, as we all know, "common sense". Of course, they are. Common sense tells us racing drivers naturally celebrate with champagne, the well-known driving aid, and that mass-market lager and football were invented the same afternoon.

The US gun industry says, "Guns don't kill people. People kill people." In the same way, the alcohol industry is saying its product is an innocent bystander. Both are, in a very literal sense, correct. People pull the triggers of guns, and people bring alcoholic drinks to their lips. But in putting it like this, both industries pin responsibility on consumers while ignoring their own. Alcohol advertising say in product placement in James Bond movies, knowingly reinforces common myths about the effects of alcohol.

The alcohol industry should not be expected to go against its own interests and go beyond the finger-pointing of the "responsible drinking" ethos. It won't. Instead, it should be prevented from fuelling the misunderstandings about alcohol's effects which foster excessive drinking. As a start, the law should be requiring clear, science-based warnings on every bottle. That would be a small step toward responsible brewing.

The research of the last 40 years overwhelmingly suggests alcohol use does our happiness and wellbeing significant harm. It is not even providing the restorative effect implied by the tag of "recreational drug". But binge drinking is on the rise, despite arguably being the most harmful drinking pattern for our brains.

The interlude between our binges is typically enough to convince us we are fine and can come to no harm. But, done often enough and for long enough, binging means we can start to find our brain chemistry become stranded in no man's land, as our brains struggle to return to equilibrium. The extra demands of trauma, like a relationship breakup or job loss, can make us drink enough to deepen dependence, which leads to a sizable dip in our feelings of wellbeing.

Northern and Eastern Europe are substantially above the global average in both total consumption and binging habits. Around 44 per cent of British men and 31 per cent of women exceed the weekly guideline amounts, which have since been cut by a third for men.[4] For many of us, a regular piss-up can be among the first things we think of when we think of work-life balance. It seems to offer a balance between work and leisure, allowing us to be sober and sensible and productive most of the time, and carefree and sociable to a deadline. This is often the core of a "work hard, play hard" lifestyle although it makes working hard more difficult, by blunting concentration, planning, and the ability to keep our cool.

Men are the most inclined to overdo it, accounting for around two-thirds of the UK's problem drinkers and 80 per cent of its dependent drinkers.[5] But this is one gender gap that is narrowing.[6] As many as 80 per cent of UK women now exceed the daily drinking guidelines meant to stop us binging, compared to 75 per cent of men. Educated women are more likely to do it.[7] Education, generally, does not preclude heavy alcohol consumption. It may partly be because our education does not include gaining an understanding of alcohol.

Such an education would begin with a very small step - Moving from giving alcohol the benefit of the doubt, as we often do, to doubting its benefit. That is all. The fact that alcohol has drawbacks, like the advice we should not drink too much, is not news to anyone. But the common sense and trial and error method we tend to use is an unfit means of navigation.

A cautious attitude has immediate advantages because moderating short and long-term consumption is a common problem. It is unlikely we are the ones who can magically drink within guideline limits without wilful effort. Over the longer term, it does not help that we often do not recognise the ill-effects of overdoing it and often do not take them seriously if we do. Anyone trying to learn something is at a serious disadvantage if they do not know when they have made an error. Also, few of us realise problems, like dependence, can result from session drinking well as steady high intake we might equate with a "real alcoholic".

Having a few days off between sessions helps, of course, but it does not necessarily clear our slate of dependency symptoms. Having no craving for alcohol in a layoff does not mean we are free of dependence or of alcohol's milder side-effects either. So, rather than assuming we escaped scot-free after a session, we could look out for symptoms like forgetfulness, emotional instability, tension, gloom, impulsiveness, sexual dysfunction, apathy, and difficulty planning. We often see these as reasons to drink more, not to slow down. Post-session discomfort of more than a day can be a sign of creeping dependence.

Dependence can steadily creep up on us unnoticed but does not leave us so easily. It takes time to get it and time to get rid of it too, typically between three months and a year. There is a significant payoff right at the start, but this initial boost does not typically rid us of all the dependency gremlins. Long as it is, recovery does not typically require group sessions or time on a psychiatrist's chair. Most of us seem to overcome it without professional help, although they are often involved in the recovery of people with additional problems in their lives. If the objective is to avoid drinking over guideline maximums, the most reliable way it seems is to stop entirely. It is harder going half way.

Maintaining a steady belief in our ability to exert control over our own behaviour is an important factor in success, whether or not others assist. This belief is, however, undermined by the unstable thoughts and feelings dependence can bring, making it harder to stick to a plan, particularly one about drinking. The well-intentioned idea of seeing dependence as a disease, which puts dependent drinkers in the role of passive victims, has the unfortunate side-effect of deflating our confidence. It is possible, however, to acknowledge the difficulties of dependence at the same time as reinforcing beliefs in our capacity to change our behaviour for our own benefit.

Alcohol's association with sociable behaviour is perhaps the bedrock of its attraction. Sociable behaviours and the feelings of connection which flow from them are proven sources of "chronic happiness", where people consistently report feeling in robust spirits. The chronically happy do not feel constantly euphoric, however. They feel resilient and have periodic rises and falls in their mood. Alcohol seems to make the resilient bounce of chronic happiness harder to achieve, instead fuelling anxiety, sleep problems, depression, and problems forming and sticking to plans.

The alcohol industry is richly rewarded for selling alcohol. In the US, it makes yearly sales of around $170 billion and, in the UK, around £38 billion ($60 billion).[8] That is an income of around 530 dollars a year per person in the US and over $900 in the UK. Such vast economic interests massively outgun those looking to provide an alternative view. Alcohol Concern, a UK charity campaigning for more responsible drinking, has an income of around £1m a year, or about 1.5p per person in the UK, around 1/45,000th that of the alcohol industry. So much for an overbearing nanny.

We willingly offer up alcohol's casualties, including ourselves, as a price which has to be paid for freedom. But freedom also allows us to question age-old hearsay, protect ourselves and others, and find new ways to pursue happiness. We do not need to rely on alcohol to be confident, relaxed and socially connected. It seems these things are likely to be more easily achieved without alcohol blunting our mood and blurring our thinking. Alcohol is rarely a life and death issue but reshaping our relationship with it still offers a rare opportunity. ∎

# Stubborn elixir

For most of human history, alcohol was a trusted companion, an essential in any western doctor's kitbag until well into the first half of last century. Its superficial sedation is seductive, still convincing many to of us to dose ourselves when we are feeling out of sorts. It is probably still dished out in modest quantities by some hospitals as a "home comfort" and as a misguided treatment for alcohol withdrawal symptoms.

Outside the body, ethanol is excellent at killing off bacteria and fungi and can also dismantle the working parts of most viruses, even tinier nasties which lurk between dead and alive. It is now generally preferred over iodine for disinfection in medical applications. Its abilities as a bug killer come thanks to its ability to breaking down the proteins which form the functional elements of living cells. Egg whites and meat do something similar when they go rubbery when cooked. Disinfectant hand gels contain around 62 per cent ethanol, and hospitals sterilise needles and other medical instruments with an ethanol solution of between 20 and 50 per cent. It can also be applied to wounds directly, at the price of a sharp sting.

People in the distant past spent most of their lives riddled with all manner of grumbling ailments for which there was little explanation and almost no realistic hope of a cure. Alcohol was one of the few readily available substances which might ease the discomfort of life for a while, even if it never solved the problem. The Greek "father of medicine," Hippocrates, who lived around 460BC, advocated wine drinking for just about every ailment imaginable, other than "an overpowering heaviness of the brain." This is one evocative diagnosis which has sadly failed to make it to the modern doctor's surgery.

Such faith in the booze remedy persisted over the centuries and perhaps reached its zenith in the "heroic cures" of the 19th century, which got their name from the need to ingest "heroic" amounts of alcohol. They were usually prescribed to people suffering from "cooling" diseases like dysentery. Prince Albert, the German-born consort to Queen Victoria, is said to have been on the receiving end of just such a courageous prescription, reputedly being told by his doctor to drink six pints of brandy a day to help him fend off the illness that finally killed him. At the time Albert was said to be suffering from typhoid, but some now suspect it was Crohn's disease, renal failure, or abdominal cancer[9]. Whatever the unfortunate prince had, it is safe to say that these prodigious quantities of alcohol would have done no great service to his health.

In lesser amounts, alcohol was seen as a balm for troubled nerves and a sleep aid. Both were understandable applications given alcohol's superficial sedative effects which help us drop off more quickly. It has lately been discovered, however, that alcohol disrupts our sleep architecture from there on.

Medics also found alcohol could act as a solvent for oily compounds which do not dissolve in water and as a preservative to prevent organic matter, like herbs, from undergoing water decomposition and fermentation. The Polish custom of flavouring vodka by steeping fruit and herbs to make a brew called *nalewka* operates on a similar principle, as does sloe gin. Alcohol's role as a preservative and solvent allowed pharmacists to extract active constituents from drug-bearing plants in their crude form. Pharmacologically-active compounds extracted this way include alkaloids, glycosides, resins and volatile oils.

These alcoholic preparations were popularised in the early 16th century by the magnificently named Swiss physician Philippus Aureolus Theophrastus Bombastus von Hohenheim, known as "Paracelsus" for short. Among Percelsus's creations was an early form of laudanum, a heady opium-infused cocktail favoured as a pick-me-up by many Victorians, including Queen Victoria herself. Laudanum, however, was only one of many potions and lotions for which alcohol provided the solvent basis. Whatever you might be prescribed, you could usually rely on having a belt with your daily dose.

Alcohol was so widely used in the hit and miss medication of the past it must have been nigh-on impossible to separate illnesses, pharmaceutical side-effects, drunkenness, hangover, and withdrawal. If your doctor followed the publican school of medicine, a long illness would have been the entrée to alcohol dependence, or a deepening of it for people who were already. The production of these alcohol-based elixirs—a word like alcohol itself derived from Arabic in which *al iksir* means a wound dressing—was widespread across Europe. It was often a sideline for monasteries which kept their recipes a closely-guarded secret, so adding a divine aura to their mysterious pick-me-ups.

Some of these quasi-medicinal mixtures contained a hundred or more different herbs, prepared according to laborious and complex procedures. Some have continued until the present day. Among the most famous survivors is the French liqueur Chartreuse, reputed to contain over 130 herbs and flowers. Others passed their sell-by-date long ago, like Warburg's Tincture, invented by German physician Carl Warburg in 1834, which set its stall out as a remedy for practically anything. A nip of Warburg's was meant to be effective against cholera, diarrhoea, and dysentery, scrofula, incipient tuberculosis, bronchitis, loss of appetite, scurvy, and "every disease of a scorbutic character", that is related to the vitamin-C deficiency scurvy. Warburg's was also employed against yellow fever, typhus, and malaria and, perhaps for those who had too much Warburg's the day before, alcohol withdrawal. The elaborate brew was prepared as follows:

*Take: 4 ounces each of Socotrine aloes, Rhubarb root (East India), Angelica seeds, and Confection Damocratric [itself an elaborate preparation]; 2 ounces each of Helenis root*

*(Elecampane root), Saffron, Fennel seeds, and Prepared chalk; and 1 ounce each of Gentian root, Zedoary root, Cubelis (tailed pepper), Myrrh, Camphor, and boletus laricis (Polyporus officinalis, a fungi). Above ingredients to be digested with 500 ounces of proof spirit in a water-bath for 12 hours; then expressed and ten ounces of Disulphate of Quinine added; the mixture to be replaced in the water-bath till all quinine is dissolved. The liquor, when cool, is to be filtered, and is then fit for use.*[10]

The pharmaceutical effectiveness of most of the elements of this blunderbuss of a preparation is extremely doubtful. But one ingredient at the very end of the list, quinine, is indeed effective against malaria. The rest, meanwhile, were liable to act as no more than a powerful laxative, a "purging" effect thought highly desirable at the time but since found to be unhelpful to the sick.

Just as booze encroached into the spiritual realm, the line between medicine and recreation was also often crossed. After all, what is meant to help the sick recover might also protect or fortify the healthy, right?

Among these crossover drinks was absinthe, a spirit infused with the flowers and leaves of *Artemisia absinthium* ("grand wormwood"), a North African herb, green anise, sweet fennel, and other herbs. The creator of the patent "cure-all", Dr Pierre Ordinaire, sold his recipe to the French entrepreneur Henri-Louis Pernod, who in 1797 ramped up production by adding a distillery in Switzerland. The brew proved so popular he opened another in Pontarlier, France eight years later. Absinthe's popularity grew further still when it was adopted by French soldiers in North Africa, who came to believe it would help stave off disease and purify their questionable drinking water. Its reputation then spread back to Paris, where it became a craze whose adherents gave the drink fantastical and sinister names, like the "Sorceress" and the "White Witch". Those more sceptical of its effects, meanwhile, called it the "Charenton Omnibus", with Charenton being the name of the local lunatic asylum.[11]

The blurring of the line between medicinal and recreational was not just a European phenomenon either. European colonists took their love of alcohol to pastures new. In North America, alcohol became the principal ingredient of many homegrown remedies which filled the gap after British patent medicines became less easy to get hold of after America's independence in 1776. There too the line often blurred between medicinal and recreational drinking. One popular drink was called Aguadiente de Taos, or "Taos Lightning", a fearsome firewater drunk by American frontiersman Kit Carson and reputed to be an antidote to rattlesnake venom. If it could counteract the effects of rattlesnake venom, then it was surely capable of much else?

Doubts about alcohol's medicinal effects steadily grew within the medical establishment over the decades. But a lingering belief survived well into the 20th century, still colouring the informal thinking of our own generation through that of our parents, by way of grandparents and great-grandparents.

Writing in the Proceedings of the Royal Society of Medicine in 1920, a William White described alcohol as a "pleasant depressant" one "peculiarly efficacious in inhibiting peripheral impulses, such as pain here, and discomfort there, that it diminishes those trivial worries which bother the sick." Another says that, "Alcohol is, I suppose, the most valuable sedative and hypnotic drug we possess for infants and young children." American doctors campaigned to be allowed to prescribe alcohol during Prohibition 1920-33. They had lost what they saw as a valuable medical tool. Brandy and whiskey were listed as drugs in the US Pharmacopeia, America's official listing of drugs, until the 1940s.

Ethanol's healing powers were thought to lie, at least in part, in its energy content which was in a pure form which invalids might ingest more readily than through normal foods. If you see how cleanly alcohol burns, with its smokeless blue flame, you can see the idea seemed to make intuitive sense. Today we might think something similar about glucose, although if you burn that it will have an unpromising dirty yellow flame. As with many wrong theories, it contains some element of truth. Alcohol does contain a lot of calories per gram, so many it is on a par with fats and oils, the richest sources of energy we have in our diets.

The heart was thought to be the main beneficiary of alcohol's clean, efficient power source, "As a circulatory stimulant, the value of alcohol is undoubted; it increases the output of blood from the heart, and slightly raises blood pressure. Its action may be due either to a direct stimulant effect on cardiac muscle, or to the fact that it affords a readily assimilable source of energy," according to an article in the British Pharmacopoeia of 1907.

Alcohol as an oral medicine fell steadily into disuse, but medical reference books continued to list it right up until the end of the 20th century. The British National Formulary of March 1997 said "where therapeutic quantities of alcohol are required, rectified spirit should be prescribed", while not going so far as to say what the therapeutic quantity of alcohol is or what it might be therapeutic for.[12] The British Pharmaceutical Industries, the association for companies producing prescription medicine, meanwhile, listed Labiton—a tincture combining alcohol, vitamin B, kola nut extract and caffeine—as having therapeutic value for postoperative convalescence.

Alcohol still clings by its fingernails to the fringes of medicine on the front line. A British teaching hospital prescribed 45 litres of alcoholic drinks a year in the late 90s, mostly being given to people over 70. There is no reason to believe it does not still go on to some extent. Guinness, sherry, and whisky were the most frequently prescribed. Around two-thirds of the nurses interviewed in the study wanted to see more alcohol prescribed by doctors, saying a drink or two improved the "home comfort" of the ward. Doctors, meanwhile, said they felt they were under pressure to prescribe more. If alcohol is being prescribed in hospital, with all its medical facilities and know-how, then it seems a racing certainty that untrained people dose themselves with a lot of something at home for whatever ails them, though possibly not against rattlesnake venom.

Even medical professionals still harbour some wildly faulty notions. Doctors in the hospital said they prescribed Guinness to help patients overcome the iron deficiency. In fact, Guinness contains so little iron that someone would have to drink 800 pints a day to achieve a therapeutic dose, far overstepping the boundary between "heroic" and definitely fatal. Doctors also said an alcoholic drink might help patients sleep. This makes "common sense", because people who have had a drink do drop off more quickly, but it is counterproductive after, as we will find out in more detail later. Prescribing alcohol might also be a help to patients who are depressed or alcohol dependent, the doctors said. Again, all the scientific evidence shows alcohol makes depression worse and only prolongs alcohol dependence. Given that alcohol is implicated in 25 per cent of male admissions to the hospital, the authors of the study, who were from the hospital's psychiatric department, said that dispensing of alcohol in a hospital sent out the wrong message. Yes, it does.

At around the same time alcohol was also being used in 11 of 32 US hospitals surveyed. In these cases, it was being used to stop the delirium and trembling some alcohol-dependent people can experience when they stop drinking. Six of the hospitals were using alcoholic drinks, mainly beer, and five intravenous injections of an alcohol solution. Some of the surgeons interviewed argued objections to prescribing patients alcohol were based on nothing more than moral and social disapproval. They also point to a textbook called Emergency Surgery, published in 1995, which said "If there is no doubt that the patient has in fact developed *delirium tremens* [spasms during alcohol withdrawal] a dose of alcohol is highly effective and can be considered". Experts in alcohol treatment agree, however, that alcohol is not the right thing to give for alcohol-induced delirium, which should be treated with sedatives known as benzodiazepines.

The authors of this second study also complained that doctors dishing out beers in a hospital gives the impression that it has medical applications it does not have. There is now only one medical situation where doctors are generally advised to prescribe alcohol use these days. That is if someone is poisoned with methyl alcohol ($CH_3OH$), ethanol's poisonous little brother with one rather than two carbon atoms. For anything else, it is off the medical menu. An improper prescription is extremely uncommon, but it shows just how deep-seated false belief in alcohol's medical utility is, even among highly-trained medics. If they cannot shake off this inherited superstition, what hope do the rest of us have?

Though alcohol is rarely prescribed these days, it still has a lingering reputation as a bringer of health. Some say regular low doses can protect us from developing heart and brain diseases, like stroke and some forms of dementia, including Alzheimer's.

This line of thought is based on very old observations. Since the turn of the last century, scientists have struggled to explain why French people do not keel over with heart disease given their rich cuisine. Statistical studies pointed to their habit of regular, low-level alcohol drinking with food as the reason. For those looking for a reason to drink, this was close to a miracle, with medicine apparently giving it the thumbs up.

On closer inspection—ignoring our wish to have a reason to drink—the news is not so great, however. Theorists tend to believe alcohol may act as a blood thinner, reducing the chances of blood clots which can clog the heart or brain.[13] This explains why alcohol alone, when stripped of its companion chemicals, seems also to have positive effects. In other studies, however, spirits drinkers have seen no benefit.[14] The bulk of the beneficial effect, then, is not the result of anything particularly profound. They are likely to be possible without ingesting a substance with alcohol's psychoactive effects or dependency.

There is a possibility that red wine, common to diets of France and the Mediterranean, may contain ingredients other than alcohol which are helping. The thinning effect may be boosted by red wine's high level of polyphenols, compounds contain a matrix of phenol molecules ($C_6H_5OH$), with resveratrol being among the favourite candidates. One study found red wine that had its alcohol removed lowered blood pressure enough to lower their risk of heart attack by 14 per cent and stroke by 20 per cent.[15] And alcohol-free beer has been shown to stop blood clotting as well as normal beer.[16]

In the meantime, there is an attempt to make French drinking habits into a permanent cultural monument. Drinking wine with food is not just tasty, fun, and arguably good for you, but of global cultural significance. The "gastronomic meal of the French", which includes the "pairing of food with wine", was honoured with the status of UNESCO world cultural heritage in 2010.[17] Three years later, the Mediterranean diets of Cyprus, Croatia, Spain, Greece, Italy, Morocco and Portugal, which also generally include moderate alcohol consumption with food, were also added to the world heritage list.[18]

The hope of an alcohol health-boost is still alive and well, then, and given UN backing, albeit for its cultural heritage. The jury is still out, however, with the answer, if there is such a thing still buried in complex statistics. There have been no randomised controlled trials. And the mechanisms behind any benefit are unclear and, again, have no conclusive trials to back them up.[19]

Critical to getting any benefit from alcohol would be getting the dose right: too little and it does not do anything; too much, and its effects are extremely counter-productive. The sweet spot appears to be somewhere between half and two standard drinks a day—the upper limit being around one-and-a-half large beers. In these amounts, it is thought to reduce people's risk of having a heart attack by around 25 per cent. Drinking six or more standard drinks a day—or more than four beers—however, seems to increase the risk.[20] Similarly, low doses of alcohol also seem to have a protective effect against stroke and dementia, albeit a smaller one. Any protective benefit is completely wiped out by occasional bingeing.[21]

And there is the rub. Since alcohol dosage is famously hard for many of us to control, particularly when taken in a pleasing form, doctors are not advised to prescribe alcohol as a preventative measure.[22] The modest doses which seem effective can easily escalate, moving into heavier drinking or session drinking, which have the opposite effect on heart and brain. These kinds of heavy drinking also bring their own problems, like anxiety, depression, and cognitive problems.

Given the fairly slender potential benefits and much larger risks, health is a questionable reason to drink. The effective amounts are below what many of us like to drink. Meanwhile, departing from the low "effective" dose can potentially result in far more immediate harm to us than may be repaid down the road. If you really want to extend your life and avoid heart and brain disease, you would be better to go for a walk in the park or take up yoga.

We are always eager for "good news" stories to confirm our affection for alcohol is not misplaced. It is nonsensical to be looking for good news in something which is bad for us in the way we like to consume it. We can worry about the threat posed by "chemicals" in our food, the perils of refined sugar, wheat, lactose, red meat, a waft of passive smoke, or plastic packaging, while polishing off a bottle of wine.

The long-standing safe drinking guidelines issued by most governments are widely considered institutional scaremongering or statistically flawed. The most plausible argument is that people tend to lie about their alcohol intake on surveys and so the official guidelines are set too low. Binge drinking, meanwhile, is generally thought of as a trick we can get away with. But the problem is that drinking guidelines have been adjusted to compensate for our tendency to underreport our intake. And binging can cause problems even if we do not notice them, which is why there are daily limits as well as weekly ones. The risks posed by alcohol are more accurately quantified than most of our dietary fears. And drinking guidelines were created largely to help safeguard us from liver disease, but there is some evidence of cognitive impairment and emotional instability at levels below guideline maximums.

The affection we have for alcohol means it is given special treatment by our politicians, who set it apart from other legal drugs. A packet of headache pills will carry blood-curdling warnings of rare side-effects, while a bottle of whisky will have practically nothing acknowledging the sure-fire harm it can cause. Providing timely and eye-catching warnings would be insulting to the "common sense" of the drinker, it is argued. So, we have to search high and low for detailed information about depression, anxiety, dependence, and emotional instability the contents may cause. By leaving us uninformed we are being flattered for having knowledge we do not have in our mind at the moment we need it. At the same time, a packet of peanuts can be relied on to warn us it may contain nuts. ∎

# Of mice and men

The thirst for alcohol goes back millions of years. Even some of the most ancient life forms, like insects, are inclined to have a tipple. Fruit flies, for example, have the capacity to build a tolerance to increasing levels of alcohol[23]. They even let boundaries slip, with hard-drinking males being more inclined to court other males[24]. It seems unlikely, however, that such anthropodic cavorting is the reason for their drinking. More likely is that there is some deep-seated attraction to ripe, sugar-laden fruit, of which the presence of alcohol is a good indicator.[25] Alcohol is not attractive because it is an inherently nice substance but most likely because it is associated with sugar, a rich source of nourishment. This link to a high-energy foodstuff is likely to be the reason for enthusiastic alcohol-seeking along the entire length of the evolutionary chain, with rats, mice, elephants, apes, and us humans coming late to the party.

Humans are by far the most able to pursue their attraction to alcohol to its logical conclusion. Only we have the high level of intelligence, technology, culture, and self-reflection needed to drink to the point it poses a risk to our wellbeing. In typical fashion, we have exploited this special gift to the full. We are, nevertheless, unwilling to allow ourselves or others to be subjected to extensive laboratory experiments, so scientists exploit the fact our nervous architecture is like that of animals. But animals' relative temperance means that they can only be induced to blood-alcohol concentrations typical of humans by spiking their food or injecting them with an alcohol solution. A new strain of lab mice which prefer alcohol to water may be a step forward in the search for an analogue, but their tiny brains mean they will never provide more than a rough comparison.[26] Try asking a mouse how it is feeling or to explain its actions? The best we can do is perform experiments on them which might, by analogy, shed some light on our own more complex behaviours.

One important difference between animals and us is that animals do not form beliefs, or at least not ones we know of. Only humans seem to reflect on alcohol and its effects on them, so they form expectations—or "expectancies" as psychologists call them—which then guide their future drinking. These beliefs have a powerful effect on our behaviour regardless of their truth. Our behaviour changes even if we are given a dud alcoholic drink, believing it to be real. No rat or mouse would be fooled by it. Being based on experience rather than on hard facts, expectations form a wavering credo, which changes in line with our drinking. Drinking more tends to raise our expectations of drinking, while drinking less tends to lower them. The maxim we seem to go by is that whatever we are doing is probably more-or-less the right idea.

Humans are also unusually sensitive to being kept locked in laboratories for long periods. The unique features of our intelligently self-destructive drinking habits can only be studied in short, small-scale laboratory experiments or when we are roaming free in our natural habitat. These two approaches provide important results, but the conclusions that can be drawn from both are limited, either by the artificiality of the lab environment or extraneous factors acting on people outside the lab. There is, then, still substantial inference always needed to apply the findings. They need to be transferred across a species barrier, from lab to real life or from a survey of individuals' experiences to a general case. ■

# Great expectations

Drinking is a choice, and like all other choices, it tends to be made on the basis that it is likely to deliver a desirable outcome. Somewhere between not drinking and drinking, we decide there is a payoff worth having. Only humans weigh up their options like this, meaning we cannot turn to rats, mice, or fellow apes for answers.

Systematic thought only plays a bit part in most drinking decisions, which are founded on expectations we have accumulated over our lifetimes. These expectations, called "expectancies" in psychologists' parlance, are a form of belief we informally acquire and pass on to others. Their transmission starts early, with parents' attitudes and behaviour rubbing off on their offspring, before the transmission process is taken up by friends, acquaintances and first-hand experience. Our differing responses to alcohol also shape our expectations, with some learning they can get a kick from drinking while some feel a bit ill or fall asleep.

Generally speaking, the more positive someone's expectations are of alcohol, the greater the alcohol-related losses they are likely to suffer during their lives. People are understandably sensitive about challenges to hard-won beliefs, particularly when they involve their faithful confidence-booster or source of anxiety relief. Expectations formed while inebriated cannot always be trusted, because inebriation can form compelling but unreliable impressions. F Scott Fitzgerald spoke of one such impression when he said, "There was a kindliness about intoxication—there was that indescribable gloss and glamour it gave, like the memories of ephemeral and faded evenings."[27] Maybe it was just so, but inebriated people tend to make inaccurate witnesses.

Despite our unique life experiences, our expectations tend to progress along a fairly common path. Younger drinkers look to alcohol as a way to boost their confidence in social situations and smooth the way to sexual liaisons. Those over 30, meanwhile, start to look to drinking as a way to manage stress.[28] Three-quarters of people say drinking alcohol makes them feel relaxed, according to a survey by the UK's Mental Health Foundation.[29] This was even more the case among people up to the age of 45, especially the ones who work. Around two-thirds of people said alcohol made them happier, while only a quarter said it made them less depressed. The same proportion of 18-24s said drinking makes them feel more confident, while just a fifth of pensioners look to alcohol to give their egos a boost.

Nationality plays a big part in what people expect from having a drink. They tend to suit the drinking patterns. Denmark and Ireland are, for example, home to the most highly-expectant young drinkers in Europe, with 40 per cent more students saying drinking was likely to result in a positive outcome.[30] The students of France, Italy, Romania and Turkey, meanwhile, expect drinking to be far less fruitful, with under 10 per cent saying the outcome of drinking would be positive. As might be imagined, the converse is also true, with the expectation of negative outcomes from binge drinking lowest where binge drinking is highest, namely in Norway, the Netherlands, and the UK.

Alcohol's chemical composition has remained exactly the same as it always has, but European expectations of it rose between 1995 and 2003. The positive beliefs do not stand up to much investigation and are linked to some self-defeating alcohol use. It tends to be those who say alcohol eases anxiety or relieves depression who drink every day, for example. Unfortunately, however, alcohol's apparent ability to ease anxiety and depression is an illusion because alcohol tends to make both problems worse, which is why no doctor would prescribe alcohol for either.

The expectation of "Dutch courage" is justified on a subjective level. Intoxication undoubtedly makes people more confident and feel more at ease. Alcohol subdues brain function meaning we are less bothered by extraneous thoughts which might intrude on an evening. We are also less bothered by reasons not to say or do something. We are able to focus more on what is happening immediately around us, helping us converse or, to some degree, dance. At the same time, the confidence that this alcohol-driven aptitude for being more present in a situation is slightly misplaced because it comes at the cost of other parts of our brain function.

And turning to alcohol to help us with a stressful challenge may be of some help, but it also has some drawbacks we may not notice. Alcohol reduces our hormonal response to stress, but it tends to extend the time we have a negative subjective experience of a stressful event.[31] So someone who has had a few drinks is likely to be unusually brave in the face of adversity, say giving a speech or singing karaoke, but is likely to feel jittery about it for longer afterwards. This latter effect is likely to go unnoticed, by all but the most perceptive of us, so the positive expectation of alcohol being an effective sedative is reinforced.

Artful marketing fuels our common expectations. Wine labels, traditionally aimed at the older drinker, might conjure up pastoral scenes of rest and ease, giving a bottle of five-quid plonk an aristocratic elan. It might, meanwhile, be suggested that supping on a traditional British ale or cider might offer us the ease enjoyed by a country squire or corn-sucking ploughman. The back of a whisky bottle may offer the chance to ingest the giddy spirit of a timeless, babbling burn, a million miles from the strip lighting and clattering trolleys of the suburban supermarket we buy it from.

A piece of vigorous contemporary graphic design on a wine label might capture the imagination of a more socially-driven drinker looking for something to pop at a party. The colourful, angular motif holds the promise of adding a bohemian frisson to ordinary life. The marketers of tequila and rum make it quite plain we can expect their product to bring wild Latin excitement to the backstreets of Bracknell or Cleveland. And a few mass-market lagers can bring us the determination and panache of our football heroes.

The atmospheric images conjured up by the drinks industry cannot be disproved. They are timeless fantasies of ease, excitement, and glory we will always enjoy and want to live for ourselves. We should not deny ourselves this need to let our minds wander from the mundane. But we are just as free to indulge in fantasy without the help of alcohol and the set-piece scenarios laid out by people who sell it. An alternative to the traditional patterns of alcohol consumption does not mean accepting austerity or dry logic. Inebriation does not make our flights of fancy any more real or our sober ones less so.

Alcohol expectations evolve during our adult life, but they do not just appear from nowhere when we hit the legal drinking age. They begin forming in childhood, even before people have had alcohol themselves.[32] We tend to start off feeling quite negative and grow more positive as we move into adolescence. Young girls seem to be less put off by alcohol use if their fathers are the ones who drink more.[33] Older children also seem to favour alcohol use by their dads, rather than their mums, where greater use tends to reduce positive expectations.

Parents and people in children's regular acquaintance play the principal role, but expectations also start to build around what we see in the media. There is no shortage of examples. For kids of the generation, their alcohol education might have started as a pre-teen with *Asterix*, a pint-sized Gallic hero who carries a hip flask containing a mysterious potion that gives him superhuman strength. Or, later, perhaps we might have seen wisecracking Benjamin "Hawkeye" Pierce, the star turn of Korean War comedy *M\*A\*S\*H*, who somehow manages to save soldiers' lives between binges on moonshine. And British TV detective Morse would crack a murder case, a crossword, and his weekly heartbreak by brooding alone with a wine rack and deafening opera. In real life, these sullen encounters seem unlikely to end in a satisfying conclusion.

The grit of the even more retro detectives played by Humphrey Bogart was only hardened by quaffing endless shots of bourbon. And innumerable cinema cowboys remained tough, hardy and priapic dead-shots despite drinking red eye like it was their last day on earth, as it often was. For the more urbane, there was the good-natured Jerry Leadbetter in 70s sitcom *The Good Life*, who thwarts the stress of work and a domineering wife with a regular dose of gin and tonic. Or Norm from sitcom *Cheers*, who props up the bar night after night yet remains affable and avuncular to the last drop. Most of the decisive action in the UK's two most-watched TV soap operas, *Coronation Street* and *Eastenders*, takes place in or around a pub. Evidently, if you do not frequent the pub, you are not part of the community.

The research on the quantity of exposure in mainstream television and cinema is outdated but offers some idea. Around 70 per cent of US primetime television programmes in the 1998-99 season included some form of alcohol drinking. Same was the case with over 80 per cent of the 100 top-grossing motion pictures between 1998 and 2002. A 2006 study found that 92 per cent of the films of the time showed alcohol use, including: 52 per cent of those classified for viewing by all ages; 89 per cent of PG films for slightly older children and more thick-skinned tots; 93 per cent of PG-13, for over thirteens; and 95 per cent of R-rated films catering specifically for adults.[34] The researchers estimated that the 10- to 14-year olds in the study had seen on average around eight hours of alcohol consumption in movies, or the equivalent of 1,000 30-second beer commercials.

And marketing extends into the physical world too. A study of 11-12-year olds in South Dakota found that 19 per cent of those who owned a hat, poster or T-shirt promoting alcohol were nearly twice as likely to drink or intend to drink as those who did not have such merchandise. Underage drinking is not just about the future, it is a lucrative business itself, accounting for nearly a fifth of consumer alcohol revenue in the US.[35]

As we grow older and our peers begin to experiment, personal experiences often start to take over what we learned from the sidelines. Generally, this comes in our early-to-mid-teens. In the US between 10 and 20 per cent of children between nine and 13 have had more than a sip of alcohol, a proportion which rises to 40 per cent by the age of 14 and reaches nearly 75 per cent among 18-year-olds.[36] Much of this exposure happens without parents' knowledge with US parents tending to know of their teenagers drinking only half the time.[37] Such sneaky drinking can often go back into earlier childhood. If you include sips rather than proper drinks, around half the US population has some experience of alcohol by the age of ten, often surreptitiously.[38] There is no evidence of whether this very low level of drinking has any impact either way. It might at least pique a child's interest and establish a new frontier of experience to experiment with.

All of it goes to create expectations. Girls are seemingly more likely to follow their friends' example than boys.[39] Heavy drinking among boys and young men, meanwhile, involves expectations which link alcohol with the risk-taking and playboy behaviour that they take to be the markers of masculinity.[40] Drinking is, in a purely practical sense, a more masculine activity, which may feed into the next generation. British men generally drink far more, reaching their peak in their mid-twenties, at around 13 drinks a week, compared to a peak of four drinks a week for women which occurs in their late thirties.[41]

"Drinking buddies", that is people whose prime purpose in our circle of acquaintances is as a drinking partner, have a disproportionate effect on our drinking habits, in part because of their influence on alcohol expectancies.[42] Such reinforcing loops add up. The more drinking buddies we have, the more drinking we are likely to do. Some enterprising researchers believe they can reduce drinking by going into colleges and challenging alcohol expectations and disrupting drinking-buddy networks.[43] It might pay to offer opportunities to find companionship outside the bar.

Another expectation people have which contributes to our alcohol drinking is in our own "self-efficacy", that is the extent to which we think we can control our behaviour. Most of us believe we have some control over our actions, but alcohol can be a challenge. Some studies show having a low belief in self-efficacy is more important than having high alcohol expectations in heavy adolescent drinking.[44] Having a low belief in your self-efficacy can make it harder to deal with the consequences of alcohol consumption too. People with higher positive alcohol expectancies and lower belief in their self-efficacy tend to have bigger problems associated with their drinking.

This leaves a paradoxical problem for those wanting to put a lid on drinking: How can we tell someone to drink less without undermining their belief in their self-efficacy? One likely reaction is that people assert their self-efficacy by doing the exact opposite. US First Lady Nancy Reagan's "Just Say No" campaign in the 80s backfired spectacularly in this way, becoming bywords for cringing conformity. Lurking beneath this rhetorical issue is the unsolved riddle of free will, which alcohol drinking brings into question. To not drink we have, somehow, to want to not drink.

We might not know what our will to drink has been as thrust on us as a plea not to. College students whose parents drink a fair bit are more enthusiastic drinkers too.[45] So, a student binge-drinker, who might look every part the feckless, self-willed rebel, is often unwittingly conforming to a set of beliefs and behaviours influenced heavily by their parents.

Our expectations change over our lifetime and can shift dramatically, both pre-figuring and reflecting changes in our drinking behaviour. Expectations have been shown to change when people complete a course of treatment for alcohol dependency[46]. A similar change in alcohol expectations is seen among people who give up or moderate alcohol under their own steam too. We can move in a stepwise manner to a new type of drinking.

It seems our brains do not become dependent on alcohol without our beliefs following them. They dutifully come along for the ride and back us up when needed. Weaning our brains off alcohol seems to turn our beliefs away from alcohol too. Changing expectations changes our behaviour, and changing behaviour changes our expectations.

This link means great effort has been put into developing ways to quantify our alcohol beliefs. There are questionnaires to measure positive and, to a lesser extent, negative expectations.[47] Can we be persuaded to change our behaviour without undermining the self-efficacy needed to do it? Providing a stream of more timely, accurate information to drinkers as they make decisions would help make it a smoother ride. Labelling would be a start in this.

So powerful are alcohol expectations that believing we have had alcohol can influence our behaviour, whether or not we have drunk anything.[48] People who wrongly think they have had a drink tend to exhibit more behaviour typical of intoxication than people who were mildly intoxicated while thinking they were sober. People with strong positive expectations that alcohol will make them relaxed and happy tend to get the biggest placebo buzz. Women feel less anxious even if they just think they have had something to drink.[49] The power of a drink goes even further than this, however. Even the mention of a few alcohol-related words is enough for us to show more group bonding[50]. Some level of fantasy is, then, part and parcel of drinking.

Our beliefs can make us feel sober too. Those of us who expect the least impairment from alcohol are the least impaired after a drink. And the same effects hold when we are given placebo drinks too. People who know what to expect can learn to be more able to overcome alcohol impairment, becoming hypervigilant when they have a drink. This learned skill is not to be confused with a real physical tolerance—although it probably is—where our brains have had enough alcohol to work better on alcohol.

Genetics also plays a part in the interplay between expectations and behaviour, with each of us getting different effects.[51] Some of us feel drowsy after alcohol, while others get more of a kick. Such apparent confirmation of positive expectancies can form a positive feedback loop, with higher expectancies increasing use and then use boosting expectancies.[52] Some have a low response to alcohol, meanwhile, and might drink more to try to achieve the positive response they see and hear about.[53]

There are outliers too. Not everybody follows the well-trodden path. Teenagers who drink alone, as some do, often do it because they believe it will help them deal with emotional problems, a mistaken idea the mind-numbing experience might reinforce.[54] They may subsequently lack the experience of dealing with emotional problems without the apparent assistance of alcohol. Lone-drinking teenagers are more likely to develop alcohol problems in later life.

Alcohol expectations also adapt to match their own body's changing reaction to it too. Alcohol-dependent people, whose brains have adapted to alcohol exposure, tend to make fewer negative associations with alcohol rather than strong positive ones.[55] Their ability to change our behaviour has significant consequences for the study of alcohol in the lab, already an environment quite unlike real life. To minimise the problem, experiments need to be done with real alcoholic drinks and with placebo drinks.[56]

Convincing alcohol placebos are not as easy to make as convincing placebo pills or injections. Who knows what an unknown pill should taste like or how an injection of a drug is meant to feel? By contrast, we are so good at detecting alcohol or its absence by taste and smell that it is nigh-on impossible to make a placebo which is guaranteed to fool us.

One method scientists use is to put a drop of alcohol on the surface of a non-alcoholic drink. The drop is too small to have any effect but does give us a familiar whiff when it is brought to our lips. Still, there is always a good chance someone will realise they have been given a dud. There is even a possibility some well-meaning subjects will pretend to have alcohol-like effects even when they know they were given a placebo, so as not to disappoint the experimenters. Creating an "anti-placebo", that is an alcoholic drink which seems like a non-alcoholic one, is more difficult still. Even a single shot is not easy to drown.

Despite these difficulties, people who have been given a placebo seldom behave exactly the same way or with the same impairments as those who have really had a real drink. The performance of people with experience of alcohol often improves after being given a placebo because they try harder in tests, suggesting they have been fooled by it to some extent. But placebo participants rarely report feeling as intoxicated as participants who really consumed alcohol. The lack of intoxicated feeling is a problem. If some subjects feel moderately intoxicated and placebo drinkers only feel mildly intoxicated, they are also likely to have different expectations of their abilities. So, a placebo drinker's mental state, expectancies, and motivations are never quite the same as intoxicated participants minus alcohol.

All this means that separating the effect of expectancies from the effect of alcohol is difficult, to say the least. But, despite the lack of a fully-convincing placebo and the natural cunning of human subjects, alcohol's effects are in good part down to what we allow it to do for us. That said, alcohol is clearly not all a delusion. The hypervigilance of people who are trying to counteract the effects of alcohol relies on parts of the brain which alcohol will sedate if enough is drunk.

Some of our expectations of alcohol arise from our low expectations of being sober, the state we choose to take leave of. If you expect to be boring, nervous or inhibited sober, it is likely you will try inebriation in the hope it might improve the outlook. It might help, then, to turn our gaze away from the downsides of alcohol at some point and to raise our expectations of being sober. Being free of its expense and side-effects is not such a bad thing. Mahatma Gandhi and reforming US president Theodore Roosevelt provide two notable examples of what can be achieved in this underrated state. To these, we might add other potential heroes like the swashbuckling Douglas Fairbanks, Nobel Prize-winning physicist Richard Feynman, escapologist Harry Houdini, and popular storyteller Stephen King. Backed by a multi-million-dollar advertising budget to match that of an alcoholic drink the expectations of this inexhaustible, free product could be drastically improved. But the question is, who would pay for it? ∎

# Neural Trojan

The liver, the organ which recycles our blood, is commonly thought to be the main fall guy of our alcohol consumption. Haggard drinkers sometimes clutch their middles and complain of feeling "liverish" after a boozy weekend. The human body produces alcohol itself, around 3g a day. Alcohol can occur naturally, and the liver has evolved to cope with it, an ability that allows us to drink. But alcohol's effect on our brains, not our liver, is the most likely cause of discomfort.

This said, processing alcohol does take a heavy toll on our livers which, over the long term, can become severe enough to seriously impair our health. Around two-thirds of the 8,416 alcohol-related deaths in England and Wales in 2013 were from liver disease, mostly of people in their 50s.[57,58] The pattern is not wildly different in other places where alcohol drinking is common. It is understandable, then, that liver damage weighs heavily on drinkers' minds.

Alcohol's relationship with the liver is fairly straight-forward when compared to the brain.[59] Gastric juices break down alcohol in the stomach, with a small amount being absorbed by the stomach wall. Up to half the alcohol is broken down by an enzyme called alcohol dehydrogenase (ADH). What remains passes from the stomach into the small intestine where it is absorbed into the bloodstream. The portal vein then carries the alcohol to the liver.

Enzymes in the liver digest as much alcohol as possible, extracting 7 calories per gram, an energy density close to the amount found in fats. But the liver misses some alcohol, and this is carried by the bloodstream into every corner of the body, including the brain. The level the blood-alcohol concentration reaches depends on the amount of alcohol. On its second pass, the same extraction process occurs, with extra alcohol being added if we are still drinking.

There are other factors at play, with food helping to slow alcohol's passage, allowing more to be broken down in the stomach. A smaller percentage of alcohol tends to be broken down in women's stomachs because they generally have lower levels of the ADH enzyme. This partially explains why women reach higher blood-alcohol levels after drinking less.

Our alcohol elimination rate can vary by as much as a factor of three depending on our genetics. Genetic factors also play a part in determining blood-alcohol concentration. Our livers have a greater or lesser capacity to break down alcohol as a result of having more or less ADH and another enzyme called aldehyde dehydrogenase, ALDH2. Asian people's livers are sometimes less efficient at it because they build up a by-product called acetaldehyde, leading to what is commonly known as "Asian flush". Apart from a red face, the unpleasant symptoms can include a headache, nausea and elevated heart rate.

Acetaldehyde is not nice stuff to have floating around, being highly reactive and toxic. It can cause tissue damage and the formation of damaging particles known as reactive oxygen species and a change in the reduction-oxidation (redox) state of liver cells. Acetaldehyde also has the capacity to bind to proteins such as enzymes, microsomal proteins, and microtubules. It is also thought to join the neurotransmitter dopamine, which plays a part in the brain's response to reward, to form salsolinol. It is thought that salsolinol might contribute to people developing alcohol dependence, although it is just one of many possibilities.[60] The liver eventually metabolises acetaldehyde to acetate most of which leaves the liver in the blood and is converted to $CO_2$ in heart, skeletal muscles, and brain cells. Another hypothesis is that that chronic alcohol use may mean the brain starts to rely on acetate rather than glucose as a source of energy.

The liver disposes of nearly 90 per cent of the alcohol which makes it into the bloodstream. But the body also disposes of tiny amounts in other ways, with some being exhaled, which is what allows for breath testing, and some comes out in our sweat. And a small amount is also extracted by the kidneys and leaves the body in urine.

Understanding alcohol's relationship with the body's supreme organ, the brain, is far more difficult. The two are clearly related but do not run in tandem. It is common to have a healthy liver function when heavily dependent. But we cannot be dependent without having problems in our brain function.

Brain function underpins our wellbeing by allowing us to regulate our behaviour, sleep, think, control our emotions, and make decisions. The brain determines our response to immediate circumstances and chooses actions with long-term consequences. As the command and control centre of our bodies, it also coordinates our unconscious functions. The liver like every other organ looks to the brain for its instructions. And, among many other things, since we are talking about drinking, the brain is the organ which puts a glass into our hand and brings it to our lips. Or does not.

Heavy drinkers have difficulty in processing information, emotional disturbances, and impaired judgement, particularly when making snap decisions. Such problems are easily missed, being written off as part of our character, or unavoidable symptoms of age or gender. Cognitive, motivational, and emotional issues are measurable quite early on in our drinking "careers" although they tend to get worse over months and years. They are largely the results of a misfiring brain.

Alcohol changes the way our brain works within seconds of having a drink. Depending on the amount drunk and the drinker's previous drinking patterns, the effects last for hours and, for heavy drinkers, possibly several days after. If an occasional drinker drinks enough in one session, they will experience a rebound, or "hangover", as the brain readjusts to having no alcohol in its tissues. This rebound will typically last for 24-

hours. But the readjustment to having no alcohol in the bloodstream takes longer if we are dependent drinkers, meaning our brains have trouble resetting after a session. These withdrawal symptoms are rarely enough to kill, although they can be in extreme cases, they invariably interfere with our ability to function.

Meddling with the way the brain works changes, to some degree, who we are. Alzheimer's and psychedelic drugs can cause people to lose their identity and show extreme changes in their thought processes. Alcohol too changes brain function in the short term, and can, if we drink enough, make structural changes which last for days, months, and years. Some of the changes, known as dependency may never completely disappear. This might change trivial responses, but can also change ones with long-lasting consequences, perhaps putting someone in conflict with their friends and family, employer, or the authorities. Alcohol disturbs our unconscious life too, disrupting the structure of our sleep when inebriated and that of dependent drinkers long after they give up.

So, rather than focussing our concern on our livers when we think about alcohol's pitfalls we should first look to the wellbeing of our brains. If we resolve to treat our brains well, a healthy liver is likely to follow.

We had this figured out a couple of millennia ago. Ancient Greek medic Hippocrates had pretty much nailed it around 400BC, "Men ought to know that from nothing else, but the brain come joys, delights, laughter and sports, and sorrows, griefs, despondency, and lamentations. ... And by the same organ, we become mad and delirious, and fears and terrors assail us, some by night, and some by day, and dreams and untimely wanderings, and cares that are not suitable, and ignorance of present circumstances, desuetude, and unskillfulness. All these things we endure from the brain when it is not healthy."

The brain's more humdrum role as regulator of bodily functions, meanwhile, was only identified only a couple of hundred years after Hippocrates, when the Roman physician Galen traced the connection between the brain, nerves, and muscles. His anatomical investigations showed how a branching network of nerves stretches from the brain to the muscles in the body.

After this promising start, western medicine veered wildly off course. The uninspiring pink blancmange between our ears was discounted as a likely candidate for the king of the organs. In the 17th century, French philosopher and mathematician René Descartes insisted that the mind existed independently of the body. But, slowly, since Descartes's time, the brain's central role in ruling the rest of the body has gradually been accepted. Even now we still have some trouble accepting all our thoughts arise from such a blob. We tend to favour the more exciting dynamic heart as our controlling organ, to which the lumpish brain plays the part of an accountant. It is probably time finally to accept the brain as our unchallenged chief executive.

Examinations of animal brains which share similar but larger component parts, like those of giant squid, were among the first to help shed light on what is going on in our miniaturised versions. Investigation of the brains of closer relations, like rats, mice, chimpanzees, and fellow humans have helped too. In the last few decades, the investigation of brains has been made easier thanks to non-invasive imaging and monitoring technologies which show what is happening in real time. Nevertheless, the details of the brain's inner workings are still sketchy, and we still do not know how our sense of "free will" fits in with the brain's obedience of physical laws. Nevertheless, we now have an unprecedented understanding of the brain and how alcohol interferes with it.

To get to grips with it, we need to consider what our brains and nervous systems do, and their similarities and differences from those of animals.

The brain is the main control unit of the central nervous system, the body's signalling network. The central nervous system carries information in and out of the brain, providing readings from our organs and senses, and carrying fresh instructions from the brain. The brain activates muscles and bodily functions, stimulating the secretion of hormones into the bloodstream, regulating the function of organs, including the brain itself. The chemistry and layout of the information network are the same in all animals, with the exception of biological oddballs, like sea squirts, sponges, jellyfish, and starfish. The shared hardware means that practically all animals have a similar response to alcohol. At its evolutionary starting point, the brain served a worm-like creature in the form of a tube with a clump of signalling cells for each body segment and the biggest at the top. Some types of worms, like leeches, are lucky enough to have two, having an enlarged ganglion at the back end, known as a "tail brain", a feature absent in humans.

The brain's response to the flow of information it receives from the rest of the body is based on inbuilt biases, or instincts. With each successive generation, the same basic template is kept, with minor changes made through the mixing of genes or errors. These biases have, according to Darwin's account, taken shape through the demise of poorly adapted variants and increased rates of reproduction of those best adapted to maximise their chance of survival. Our brain's response is also influenced by the outcome of similar flows of information in its living past, allowing us to learn and cope better with situations which occur more than once.

By and large, animal brains get bigger or smaller in line with the mass of the body they manage, although smaller animals tend to have slightly larger brains in proportion to their body weight. But, still, mice have small brains to control their small bodies, and elephants have big ones to serve their big bodies. Factors other than bodyweight play a role in relative brain size too, with predators seeming to need a bit of extra nous per pound of flesh to earn their keep, as do specialist aeronauts like hummingbirds. Primates too have unusually big brains for their size, with humans being the most extreme example.

One measure of braininess in mammals is the "encephalisation quotient", or EQ, a variable which attempts to eliminate the brain-swelling effect of body size. While far from perfect, it shows just how unusual humans are. On this scale, humans score between seven and eight, while most other primates manage just two-to-three. Dogs are around 1.2, while the mice and rats, the primary medical model used in alcohol and other medical research, hover around a measly 0.5. The growth of human brains is not a one-way process, however, with evidence from fossilised remains of human ancestors suggesting brains have shrunk by 10 per cent in size over the past 28,000 years.

Apart from their raw size, human brains' other unique feature is their efficient use of space. They are very crumpled, increasing the size of the outer layer, called the cortex. This is important because the outer layer seems to be where most activity takes place. When unfolded, the two cerebral cortexes of a human brain, one left and one right, have a surface area of 0.24 square metres, around the size of a pair of dinner plates. Each of these outer layers operates on up to half-a-dozen separate sub-layers. The human cerebral cortex is so large that it dominates the working of every other part. Again, however, humans are not unique in having a very crinkly cortex, with dolphins and whales having even more convoluted ones still, although their brains are only half as big in terms of EQ.

It is a costly business running a brain because they consume a lot of power. Compared to the rest of the body, brains use over 16 times more energy per kilo. This tends to keep their size down. Animals typically devote between 2 per cent and 8 per cent of their energy on fuelling their brains, while the human brain gobbles up as much as 25 per cent. This is an extraordinary premium for an organ which, at a weight of 1.5kg, might typically only make up around 2 per cent of our bodyweight.

The investment of energy we make in our brains is a measure of its importance to our survival. Our capacity for learning is far greater than other species, making us adaptable to changing circumstances. We are likely to be the only species with the same level of self-awareness. We also have an unusual capacity for abstract thinking and reason, communication and culture, and with it the capacity to record and cling on to both truths and falsehoods.

The unique complexity of our brain is a problem when trying to study its function, like higher forms of cognition and language. It is considered unethical to disable or stimulate parts of a person's brain to see what happens. So, scientists have to study people who have lost parts of their brain through misfortune or use animals, most often the hapless mouse or rat. On the upside, however, humans' capacity to cooperate means some special types of investigation are possible on humans. A subject can be asked to do something while researchers monitor the blood flow in their brains, using a range of techniques called "functional neuroimaging". They might also monitor electrical activity in the cortex using electrodes on the scalp, a technique known as "Electroencephalography".

Research into alcohol is, nevertheless, seriously hampered by the restrictions on studying the animal it affects the most, humans. Animal experiments are useful, but the inferences that can be made from them also have limits because we differ significantly. A rat which has its entire cerebral cortex removed, for example, is still able to walk around and interact with the environment. A person with the equivalent level of cerebral cortex damage would be in a permanent coma. So, while human brains are part of the family of animal brains, from which much can be learned, they are also a special case within it.

Human brains have several unusual characteristics which point to a reason for its capacity for higher-level reasoning. There is, however, nothing completely outlandish about them either. So, if one asks, "What magical trick makes us intelligent?" as cognitive scientist Marvin Minsky asked himself in his 1989 book *The Society of Mind*, "The trick is that there is no trick. The power of intelligence stems from our vast diversity, not from any single, perfect principle."

Humans are not unique in being partial to a tipple either. But our extreme nervous architecture seems to make us liable to drink to a level which causes serious damage to our well-being, a behaviour not seen in other species. No chimp has yet been seen founding a brewery. Less intelligent animals have to be force-fed alcohol or injected with it to achieve blood-alcohol levels typical of a heavy human drinker. This is perhaps not too surprising since many brain diseases and psychiatric conditions are also unique to our brains. There is, it seems, a heavy price to pay for pushing brain technology so hard.

Alcohol drinking has also woven itself into our lives providing a social function, a source of reflection, ritual, fantasy, currency of exchange and commerce. We can also believe it makes us bolder and more relaxed. These outside influences all change our drinking behaviour, but at the heart of it all, are our brains.

Brains' softness makes them tricky to handle. Physical examination is only possible after they are steeped in chemical "fixatives" to stiffen them. Ironically, perhaps, one of the most common fixatives is alcohol, which takes apart the brain's proteins, making the tissue rubbery and so easier to cut and handle.

After fixing, brain tissue can be separated into two types: a darker one, known as "grey matter", a pinkish colour before it is fixed; and inside there is the lighter-coloured "white matter", a very light pink before it is fixed. While still alive, these delicate tissues lie within a high-security zone to keep out bugs and toxins, sealed off from the bloodstream by especially dense blood vessel walls. This creates what is known as the "blood-brain barrier". Alcohol, like all other psychoactive drugs, crosses to the brain, changing the way the brain operates and so our behaviour.

Delving deeper still, the brain is far from being an undifferentiated blob, although its parts are not laid in an orderly fashion, as in a computer. The main features of the layout are shared by different types of animals, although their shape and size vary from one species to another. Some parts, such as the cortex, the brain's outer skin-like layer, are crumpled up into deep valleys and tight folds. Other important parts, such as the thalamus and hypothalamus, are tiny clusters of cells. The size of a region has little to do with the relative importance of what it does.

It has been found that different areas of the brain specialise in different things, largely by observing the limitations of animals and people missing particular bits. Many of these tasks do not correspond to things for which we have everyday words, being either unconscious processes or subsidiary elements of a mental process.

Structural and chemical differences allow anatomists to divide the brain into six main regions, and then into thousands of more distinct areas, each given a tricky Latin name. We need not remember them, but a few key parts of the brain are:

*Medulla*: runs along the spinal cord and is involved in sensory and motor functions.

*Pons*: in the brainstem at the bottom of the brain, is on top of the medulla, controls sleep, respiration, swallowing, bladder function, equilibrium, eye movement, facial expressions, and posture.

*Hypothalamus*: a small but important structure regulating functions including sleep, eating, drinking, and hormone release.

*Thalamus*: controls a diverse range of functions, including the relaying of information to and from the cerebral hemispheres, motivation, eating, drinking, defecation and sex.

*Cerebellum*: modulates the outputs of other brain systems to make them precise.

*Optic tectum*: allows actions to be directed toward points in space, most commonly in response to visual input.

*Pallium* or "grey matter", is called the cerebral cortex in mammals where it dominates the brain.

*Prefrontal cortex*: the part at the front of the brain which accounts for most of the extra brain mass seen in human and other primates, mostly responsible for vision. Perhaps more importantly, however, it also plays a crucial role in planning, working memory, motivation, personality, attention and resolving conflicting thoughts, of which there is more later. It takes up a far larger proportion of the brain for primates than for other species, and an especially large fraction of the human brain.

*Hippocampus*: gets its name because it looks like a seahorse, is found only in mammals. It appears to have a role in forming long-lasting "episodic memories", which are those which record specific events.

*Basal ganglia*: sends inhibitory signals to all parts of the brain which can generate motor behaviours and in the right circumstances can release the inhibition. Reward and punishment situations have their most significant impact in the basal ganglia, changing its structure.

Seeing the structures within these different areas takes another chemical treatment which turns different tissues to different colours. Under the microscope, this reveals the structure within. What can be seen are branching cells, the neurons, which look like potatoes that have started sprouting. The neurons are surrounded by a roughly equal number of another type of cell, called "glial cells", which keep the neurons apart, and provide them with nutrients.

But most of the space in the brains of more complex animals, like mammals, is taken up by the wiring, the extension of the sprouts from each neuron. There are around 175,000 kilometres (110,000 miles) of axon connections in a human brain, around half the length of all the roads in the UK packed into every human head. These connections are often bundled together in nerve fibre tracts which are wrapped in fatty insulating sheaths of "myelin", which is what gives the white matter its lighter colour.

The whole system is electrical. Each neuron emits pulses of electricity, each lasting less than a thousandth of a second, about a fifth of the time taken for a housefly to beat its wings. Their level of activity varies widely, with some emitting very fast irregular pulses, up to 100 times a second, while others lie dormant much of the time. The pulses are transmitted at up to 350 kilometres an hour down the thin, branching axon fibres, to an average of 7,000 other neurons, both near and distant. The combination of electrical signals entering each neuron determines whether it pulses, some inputs stimulate a neuron to fire while others restrain it. The neuron's output signals may also be carried straight to distant parts of the body to regulate a bodily process.

It may sound like a chaotically-wired meat computer, full of elaborate pulsing transistors. But it is not that simple by a long way. There is another element in this vast jumble of interconnected nodes. Between axons and the often thousands of neurons with which they connect are sealed units containing gaps, called "synapses". When the electrical signals from neuron reach a synapse, they trigger the release of chemicals trapped in the synapse, called neurotransmitters. This, again, happens at lightning speed. It is this release of neurotransmitters which carries the signal across the synapse and then to a neuron. Psychoactive drugs, like alcohol, have their effect on the brain by disrupting the operation of these synapses which influence the pattern of neuronal firing.

Synapses are not just bit players in brain activity. Synapses have a stranglehold on the flow of information, tightly managing the flow of traffic. To get an idea of how overriding they are, we could imagine scaling the brain up and taking a road trip along the axons, with neurons being junctions and synapses the traffic lights. In the UK, there are 25,000 traffic lights regulating 344,000 kilometres of road, meaning a vehicle will pass a traffic light every 14 kilometres. As mentioned above, the human brain's connecting axons span half the distance of the UK's roads, but their traffic is regulated by 87 quadrillion synapses, an average of around 1,015 for each of its 86 billion neuron junctions. This means there is a synapse intervening in a signal's journey every thousandth of a millimetre. Neurons, by contrast, are a relatively uncommon feature, occurring only every 11 millimetres, 11,000 times less often than synapses. Fruit flies' brains, about the size of a grain of table salt, are also beholden to the synapse. There are 10 million fruit fly synapses directing traffic between its 200,000 neurons. Simple worms have just 302 neurons but still have 7,500 synapses.

Synapses regulate signals in different ways, with some suppressing the neurons on the receiving end and others stimulating them. The sum of the different inputs a neuron receives, often in the hundreds or thousands, will determine whether it puts out an electrical pulse of its own. The number of variables which decide whether a neuron fires means even a single one can deliver a complex range of outcomes, which it might require a network of dozen transistors to simulate. And the behaviour of a neuron is also not fixed over time like the dependable transistor but will give a different output depending on metabolic factors.

The response of synapses is not fixed over time either, depending on the pattern of signals which have previously flowed through them. Learning and memory is founded on this activity-dependent modification of synapses, with synapses adapting to the rewards and punishments that result from a given action. Consequently, modifying the way a synapse functions alters an animal's learning and recall. Animals learn to take drug when synapses adapt to associate it with what seems like a positive outcome. Here we are talking about a kind of unconscious learning, not like learning the rudiments of algebra or irregular Latin verbs. It is the kind of learning that also happens when we drink alcohol too.

But just when we might think we had reached the final complication, another layer of complexity appears. The brain's synapses, which regulate the signals entering neurons use dozens of different neurotransmitters, each of which tends to have different effects on the neuron receiving them and are sometimes associated with different brain areas.

Neurons tend to release the same chemical neurotransmitter, or combination of neurotransmitters into all the synapses which connect it with other neurons. This seldom-broken rule is called "Dale's principle". The type of neurotransmitters a neuron discharges is, therefore, a reliable way of categorising neurons. The neurotransmitter serotonin, for example, seems to play a role in regulating mood, appetite, and sleep, and found exclusively in synapses in a small brainstem area called the Raphe nuclei.

The most common neurotransmitters are: glutamate, which makes it more likely the neuron receiving will fire; and gamma-aminobutyric acid (GABA), which makes the firing of the receiving neuron less likely. On account of their different effects, they are called "stimulating" or "inhibitory" neurotransmitters, respectively.

Alcohol has some near-universal effects on neurotransmitters in nearly all brains.[61] It boosts the level of the inhibitory neurotransmitter GABA, reducing brain activity, giving us a feeling of calm.

It also slows parts of the brain which control muscles, meaning we are less twitchy, which is why small amounts of alcohol steady our hand. It is effective enough at this to mean that National Collegiate Athletic Association and World Anti-Doping Agency added alcohol to their list of banned performance-enhancing drugs in 2009, along with beta blockers, to stop people getting an advantage in sports like shooting.[62] In sufficient quantities, however, alcohol's GABA suppression can disable the part of the brain responsible for balance meaning we fall over.

Alcohol's other universal effect on us is lowering the release of glutamate. This lack of stimulating glutamate is what accounts for the "memory blanks" because glutamate is linked to short-term memory and its absence will stop us from creating them. Reduced glutamate release in the dorsal hippocampus, the part of the brain taking care of navigation, can also lead to spatial memory loss, meaning we are also more likely to get lost when inebriated.

The neurotransmitter imbalances caused by alcohol will disappear if someone who rarely drinks it lets their alcohol level drop. This is because the brain has a self-regulating mechanism called "homeostasis", which means the levels of neurotransmitters drift back to levels where brain activity goes back to normal again.

If someone has drunk enough, there may be a painful transition phase we recognise as a "hangover", which last up to 24-hours. But everything does not always return to exactly as it was, however, binge drinking can leave behind some deficiencies in cognitive and emotional functioning. And, if you regularly drink a lot, the brain's attempt to achieve homeostasis will make it adapt, so its activity level is closer to normal when there is alcohol present. It does this by making neurons less sensitive to the sedating GABA neurotransmitter and increasing sensitivity to glutamate. This is one of the fundamental changes of dependency.

This change in neurotransmitter sensitivity is likely to mean we will suffer after the hangover, because our neurons are insensitive to the calming effect of normal levels of GABA and extra-sensitive to the stimulating effects of glutamate. The effect of this is the reverse of the calm, forgetful state of inebriation, making life tense and vivid. It could be as dramatic as seizures and hallucinations, but in milder cases, it is likely to be anxiety, trembling, nausea, sweating, and insomnia.

Alcohol is far from being a precision neuro-pharmaceutical, however. It has been found to meddle in the transmission and receipt of other neurotransmitters including the cannabinoid, opioid, and dopamine receptors. It is unclear, however, if these changes happen because of the presence of alcohol or as a knock-on effect of changes in GABA and glutamate levels. From the drinker's point of view, it does not matter if the effects are primary or secondary. They still happen. As with GABA and glutamate, if levels of other neurotransmitters are disrupted while drinking, the brain will try and return them to normal after. If we drink enough alcohol for long enough, equilibrium may be hard to reach.

A single heavy session is enough to dull some cognitive and emotional responses for a few days or weeks. And a more concerted drinking programme can mean our brain becomes over-sensitive or deaf to key neurotransmitters, altering our feelings, thoughts, behaviour, and body functions, including sleep. ■

# First contact

We generally start life with a blank slate, simply observing alcohol use by others. Unless our mothers drank heavily while they were pregnant with us, our own journey only starts for real with our first drink.

Some of this glow that comes with having our first drink is, doubtless, the heady combination of mischief, novelty, and feeling grown up. But compounding these feelings are feelings brought on by the effect of alcohol on our brains. There is no predestined course, but such positive early impressions are difficult to erase. Some deep, lifelong memory of alcohol's potential to deliver a good feeling can be laid down which is not easily erased. Even some genes might begin to be expressed differently after, as they are in fruit flies after a single alcohol exposure.[63] Despite alcohol providing an entry ticket to the grown-up world among humans, there is nothing inherently grown up about a taste for it. Infant rats are happy to accept an elevated blood-alcohol level.[64]

It is quite common for parents to introduce children to drinking wine with a meal. The theory goes it is better to introduce children to alcohol in an easy-going way, without building it up into something to be revered or feared. It can be presented as one of life's pleasure. It is a nice idea, but it also ignores a fundamental difference between alcohol and most other pleasures. Alcohol involves a psychoactive drug which does not allow us to weigh it easily against other things. Playing a sport or listening to music does not have the same effect on the brain's inner workings.

For all the good intentions supervised drinking may, in fact, inspire rather than restrain unsupervised drinking. A Dutch study found that teenagers who drank at home were more likely to drink outside the home too.[65] Drinking in many people's early life is often exclusively associated with festivity, be it a Sunday lunch, Christmas, wedding, or some other get-together. Amassing positive early associations of alcohol consumption is not necessarily helpful if we wish to develop an approach to alcohol truly our own. Not all children are keen to follow our example, however. Around a third of 10-14-year-old British children say they are scared when they see adults drinking:[66]

Instilling a moderate, French-style approach to drinking is difficult outside France. British teenagers are not likely to prepare a wholesome evening meal and drink a glass of red wine. The focus is more on obtaining large amounts of alcohol, drinking it, and messing around. This largely clandestine activity is more about collaborating to breaking the rules, rather than playing nicely within them. Such experimentation is taken to be a normal part of growing up.

It ignores our optimistic nature. Presented with two choices which are not apparently mutually exclusive, that is the appreciation of drinking moderately and of drinking large amounts, we might well choose both. There is fundamentally nothing to stop us combining a continental European attitude to drinking as an accompaniment to food, with the traditional beer guzzling typical of northern Europe. It is the best of both worlds unless you are attempting to drink below guideline limits.

The key to the typical Southern European habit of drinking sparingly may not be so much born of appreciation of moderate drinking, but scorn for those who drink too much. This kind of intolerance is uncomfortable for northern Europeans to instil when they are not genuine, having been brought up in cultures which celebrate heavy drinking.

Social and cultural circumstances make the effects of exposure difficult to disentangle. But a fairly simple story emerges which is that early alcohol exposure does not seem to help us become better drinkers, like early cello or French lessons can improve our abilities in those areas. Instead, earlier exposure seems to prime us to develop alcohol problems later in life.[67]

Adolescent rat drinkers consumed more alcohol when they were adults.[68] And there is a similar pattern in people too. In one US survey, almost half of people who had become alcohol dependent started drinking at 16 or younger, compared to a quarter of all drinkers in the survey. Put another way, the risk of developing alcohol dependence decreases by around 14 per cent for each extra year later someone drinks.[69] An earlier survey found people who started drinking before 15 were four times more likely to develop alcohol dependence than those who began drinking at 21.

The survey also found drinking problems can often start early, with almost half of those who ended up with drinking problems already showing signs of alcohol dependence—that is withdrawal symptoms—by the age of 21. The earlier we start drinking, the higher the risk we have of episodes of drinking problems and a wider range of symptoms. The link held even after researchers attempted to remove other risk factors associated with developing drink problems, like drinking because of depression, having parents with alcohol problems or some genetic predisposition to alcohol.

Our genes play a big part, however. Studies on mice suggest that there are likely to be many genes which change the way we deal with drinking.[70] But two types of mice have been found which differ quite markedly in their affinity for alcohol, with the ones preferring alcohol known as p mice and the others non-p mice. They have around 4,000 differences in the expression of their genes, making finding the ones responsible for their differing alcohol consumption like finding a needle in a genetic haystack. The painstaking search has now been reduced to 75 prime candidates, some of which seem to be associated with human alcohol problems too.

Other rodents also fall into two camps when it comes to alcohol too. In 2013, scientists found that rats which are drawn to alcohol have a severely dysfunctional form of the gene for a receptor in the brain.[71] More specifically metabotropic glutamate receptor 2 (Grm2) does not work properly in alcohol-preferring rats but works okay in rats which are not natural born drinkers. The link was confirmed by blocking the receptor with drugs and making genetic changes to increase alcohol consumption in normal rats and mice.

Similar genetic hand-me-downs seem to guide our drinking habits too. The children of alcohol-dependent people are four times more likely to become alcohol dependent than those who are not. And the children of people who have the signs of alcohol abuse—without necessarily being dependent—are more likely to be alcohol abusers.[72] There is still a greater risk of alcohol dependence if someone is brought up by an adopted parent too, so it is not to do with bad habits. Identical twins too have a much higher rate of both becoming dependent on alcohol if one of them is dependent, as compared to non-identical twins.

Genetics and early exposure seem to bias people's behaviour towards problematic alcohol drinking. Some of us are drawn into orbit, as if by a gravitational pull, while others can break free relatively easily. But it is currently only possible for us to guess if we have risky genes. We can, however, look to our parents and siblings as a guide and take precautions, just as people do who have a family history of heart disease or cancer.

We can also see the perils of a competitive approach to life. People who have a low brain response to alcohol sometimes drink more to try to experience the effect it has on their more responsive drinking companions.[73]

Humans would not be the only species to have a group among them relatively impervious to booze, although they are the only ones to respond by trying to overcome the affliction. Fruit flies thrive on rotting fruit and so are attracted to alcohol. It also makes them inebriated, at low doses increasing their activity, while in higher doses it has a sedative effect.[74] Some of them, however, are much more resistant to the sedative effects than others, moving around for much longer after alcohol exposure. The key difference in them is a gene which also reduces their sensitivity to other psychoactives like cocaine and nicotine.

This gene's potential link to a penchant for a range of drugs inspired the research team to call it "White Rabbit", after the haunting 1967 Jefferson Airplane song about a surreal Alice in Wonderland world entered by someone popping hallucinogenic pills. It opens with:

*One pill makes you larger*
*And one pill makes you small*
*And the ones that mother gives you*
*Don't do anything at all*

To reflect the results of the experiment more accurately, however, the song would need to be rewritten slightly. The ineffectiveness seems to be the fault of your mother's genes rather than the pills you are given.

There are other genetic differences which change our drinking behaviour. Some of us have a twitchy nervous system which we initially find alcohol soothes, only to later discover the effect does not work indefinitely.[75] Another genetic link has been made to a kind of receptor in the brain's reward system which helps us learn what to do.[76] Another study found that people who feel a bigger "beer buzz" at college are more likely to develop problems with drinking later on in life.[77] Just a whiff of alcohol is enough to turn on the reward centres of some people while it leaves others cold.[78]

There also appears to be a connection between being drawn to nicotine and alcohol. The strain of rat which likes alcohol also takes twice as much nicotine as rats which do not feel the siren song of alcohol.[79] In humans too smoking is around three times more common in alcohol-dependent people as in the general population.

Some people are more sensitive to the giddiness alcohol can deliver, among them are those with a "mu-opioid receptor variant" called 118G. They report greater feelings of euphoria after consuming alcohol than those with the more common 118A.[80] It is not a particularly rare thing, with around 25 per cent of white people having the alcohol-preferring 118G variation[81]. The giddy feeling comes because of a spike in the release of a neurotransmitter called dopamine, detected in humans using positron emission tomography (PET). The human 118G or 118A variants can also be put into mice and the difference in dopamine response measured. Mice equipped with the 118G variant showed peak dopamine four times higher than mice with the 118A variant. This huge difference makes the experience quite different.

Monkeys can naturally have 118G receptor variants like us. They also respond more enthusiastically to alcohol, consuming significantly more than ones with the 118A variant.[82] Given access to both alcoholic and non-alcoholic solutions for an hour a day for six weeks, monkeys with the 118G variant became more active, which is thought to correspond to pleasure, while males with it were particularly likely to go overboard. Males with the 118G variant got inebriated on almost 30 per cent of testing days, more than three times the frequency of that of animals without it. Similarly, people whose brains release more dopamine are also found to feel less sedated by alcohol.[83]

People with the 118G variant tend to have more difficulties controlling their drinking.[84] According to one study, those with it are three times more likely to report family alcohol problems.[85] Alcohol-dependent people with the 118G variant also reported getting a greater relief from the discomfort of not drinking, so increasing the emotional ups and downs of dependence.[86] Another indicator of 118G's significance is that people with it have a better therapeutic response to medications which block opioid receptors.

Another genetic factor has been found through another much-studied animal species, college students. This variant is linked to the neurotransmitter called serotonin.[87] Students with a variation of the serotonin transporter gene called 5HTT consumed more alcohol in a session and more often had the explicit goal of getting drunk. Serotonin is linked to a role in regulating mood, appetite, and sleep, as well as cognitive functions like memory and learning.

Alcohol could be one area where starting late and not being allowed to study it too intensely is the best start we can have. Passing on a basic understanding of what it does might also help. ∎

# Bottled desire

One thing rats, mice, and even apes cannot tell us is what it feels like for them to be inebriated. It is likely that they not only lack the words to tell us, but the brainpower to reflect. Together with different lifestyles and range of interests, this means they can only ever provide clues about our drinking behaviour.

No other creature voluntarily drinks to the same level as people do. This is not because animals are too wise, but the reverse. Other animals do not drink to destruction because they do not have the wit to do so. Self-destructive alcohol use is the unique achievement of the world's most sophisticated brain, uniquely able to take practically any behaviour to its logical conclusion. But we do have the ability to understand things beyond our direct experience, or even in conflict with our direct experience, and to change our behaviour accordingly.

It does not take most people long to realise that alcohol can fall short of its apparent promise. Yet it remains just as convincing. People whose brains release an unusually large amount of dopamine when they drink, like those with the 118G receptor variant, are particularly likely to be taken in, because in normal life dopamine release is the marker of a rewarding experience. This chemical carrot-dangling means we can see alcohol as offering a colourful and reliable source of satisfaction, despite experiencing evidence to the contrary.

When badly directed, we can find ourselves on a path where the rewards are not what we thought they were or where we harm ourselves. The dopamine response can mean alcohol flashes a sign saying, "Good times this way," when there is nothing to back it up. Following a path of perpetual letdowns is not for the idle or lazy, particularly when the aftereffects of inebriation make daily life more challenging. For people who have developed dependency, or if alcohol fuels anxiety and depression, an ordinary day can seem like a mountain, with minor obstacles presenting difficulty, worry, and even terror.

This is not a route for people looking for an easy life. But our admiration for such endurance has to have limits because it is often unintended. Alcohol's long history and comforting marketing give us trust in what is essentially a cheap "street drug" with a long history. Our misguided trust means we tend to miss the downsides or see them as an unavoidable fact of life. A more sceptical view would be more successful in avoiding the pitfalls. It would be more reasonable to assume any sleep disturbance, anxiety, depression, or forgetfulness could be being fuelled by heavy drinking, rather than hoping they are not. Depression, ironically, is among the main factors which make people who quit return to drinking, only to make it worse.[88]

Apart from the cash expense, the hangover is the most blindingly obvious item on the cost side of any alcohol cost-benefit calculation. Most people will tend to think of it as a morning, or possibly a day of discomfort, paid in exchange for a night of jollity. But the effects of a heavy session can extend beyond a single morning, with remnants of dysfunction lurking much longer. The classic weekly binge can still mean cognitive dysfunctions and emotional instability while laying the foundations of dependency. Alcohol boosts the brain's capacity for habit formation while hampering the parts to do with making more complex decisions.[89]

As individuals, we find it hard to see the effect, but the pattern is clear in large population samples: alcohol consumption generally makes life less enjoyable. We are sacrificing happiness without realising. A 15-year study of Finnish identical twins—a sample chosen to rule out genetic component—found that alcohol use was associated with life dissatisfaction.[90] Binge drinkers, meanwhile, are more liable to suffer from depression.[91] It seems alcohol temporarily blocks out difficult thoughts, only to let them rush back in with greater force after. Around 3 per cent of those who drink very heavily experience the paranoia or hallucinations of psychosis while drunk or during withdrawal.[92] Around one-in-ten heavy drinkers and dependent drinkers experience severe withdrawal symptoms, including psychosis.

We might want to get "out of their mind" only to find ourselves a prisoner of it.

There are also some effects of alcohol which we might miss as casual observers, which most of us are. Alcohol seems to inhibit the ability to suppress fear, one of our most powerful emotions. In one experiment, mice were played a tone before being given a painful electric shock through their feet. After a while, the mice put two and two together and start to show a fear response when they hear the tone. But mice given large doses of alcohol continued to show the fear response to the tone long after the electric shocks had stopped. This is a lack of learning-power known as "fear extinction".[93] It seems likely that you do not need to be a mouse to have difficulties accepting the coast is clear, which would be one explanation for anxiety, perhaps something we could see as a kind of slow-burning fear. Despite apparently initially appearing to relieve anxiety and boost bravado, actually fuels it for the long term.

So, what of "Dutch courage", the idea that being half cut will make us brave? Initially, it does seem to work. Rats injected with alcohol the first time were indeed bolder than sober ones, spending more time in the riskier, exposed areas of a maze. But their courage proved to be a limited resource. Once made alcohol dependent their confidence evaporated. Even dependent rats which have been sobered up still spent more time in the safer closed sections than normal ones.[94] This effect is more pronounced in strains which are drawn to alcohol and appear to use it as a stress reliever. Alcohol-preferring rats" were more timid to begin with and, after having been exposed to alcohol, seem more so when stressed out after sobering up.[95]

The main barrier to understanding alcohol, apart from a reluctance to spoil a good party, is its inherent complexity. It modifies the workings of a complex organ, the brain, in ways which vary from one person to the next. It is not surprising, then, that the effects tend to go unrecognised.

Alcohol-related problems are not like having a broken arm, where a diagnosis is clear cut. It is always possible to attribute our problems to some cause. We can tell ourselves we feel down because we argued with our partner or because the weather is bad, or because the Wi-Fi is broken. And, to further confuse the issue, some of us may have problems at considerably lower alcohol intakes than others. And problems we might experience can also be related to our particular circumstances. Cognitive and emotional limitations can be no problem in some situations, but not in others. And, as we know, a bust-up, bereavement, or job loss can sometimes dramatically change our circumstances overnight.

A worsening of circumstances and of mood can increase the emotional forces which might make us want to drink alcohol. Alcohol can heighten these forces, relieving anxiety and depression only to increase it afterwards.

For those of us whose dopamine system is fired up by alcohol, it dangles a flashing chemical-carrot to guide us towards it, advertising alcohol's rewarding goodness. So, it is worth investigating what this dopamine release might actually feel like.

While dopamine is commonly called the "pleasure neurotransmitter", it does not seem to deliver pleasure. Instead, it seems to be connected to the perceived importance of a possible future course of action, or its "salience", to use the jargon.[96] Dopamine is involved in the expectation of pleasure, rather than its delivery with its level tending to peak before something is consumed not during it. Adding salience to an activity makes it seem important, rather than increasing the pleasure of it. This seems a likely cause of confusion.

The salience of having another couple of drinks might explain why it is given priority over an activity more likely to deliver pleasure the following day. It could perhaps be looked at as the feeling of "wanting" something rather than liking it. It is perfectly possible to want something without liking it. This seems quite typical of an alcohol drinking session which has gained a self-perpetuating head of steam. In these situations, we might find ourselves ordering a drink we know we will not enjoy. How many times has someone wrinkled their nose at a drink they just ordered at the end of the night?

Rodents provide some potentially helpful insight. Rats which have had the dopamine removed from their brains are physically able to eat but do not do so, even when they have food right in front of them. They do not want the food, so they do not eat it, even though they may still get pleasure from it. The rats do not give salience to eating and so do not do it. Dopamine highlights a rewarding activity on the radar rather than providing a pleasurable payoff. When dopamine is doing its job properly, it gives us, and rodents, the capacity to home in on rewarding events based upon previous experience. If it is released at the wrong time, however, we might start to pursue unrewarding things, like the one for the road.

Dopamine is, then, a desire transmitter rather than the pleasure neurotransmitter. It might not give us the buzz itself but is essential to alerting us to what is likely to pay off. A purely hedonistic life, guided only by immediate pleasure, would lack all direction and rationale. Without a desire for the unpleasurable but ultimately rewarding action, there would be no way for us to commit time and energy to activities other than, perhaps, tickling ourselves. Work, for instance, is frequently not pleasurable but is still desirable. It is impossible to form any kind of chain of action without the ability to generate a desire to get to the next step.

Liking, meanwhile, is not a reward in itself. Something that is liked only becomes something that is pursued when it has dopamine attached. Similarly, wanting something without liking it, like the drink we order at the end of the night "without thinking", is a kind of dopamine knee-jerk action. You can make rats behave similarly by electrically stimulating their lateral hypothalamus to release dopamine. They then want food without showing the normal signs of liking it when they eat it. It will look very much like normal reward-seeking behaviour if you do not notice the rat's lack of satisfaction after.

The sensation of "liking", meanwhile, seems to be influenced by different neural systems, including the GABA systems in the brain stem, which alcohol also stimulates. This feeling of liking and the wanting are perhaps being connected by alcohol, rather than by a more tangible payoff.

Finding the words is difficult at this level of brain activity. The words "want" and "desire" are, perhaps, too suggestive of positive outcomes. Our actions are not all about achieving positive ends. We can also act to avoid the negative. Dopamine plays a role here too, helping rats escape uncomfortable situations.

Rats which have their dopamine systems artificially depleted will not flee from danger. So, we might say in this case dopamine release seems to help establish the importance of taking steps to achieve the goal of finding safety. But there can also be an unexpected emotional crossover between desire and fear: At some point, the flow of dopamine highlighting the importance of making an escape can reach a point where rats perceive it as frightening. In humans, this flip from desire to feeling of fear could explain how a dopamine overflow could play a part in the paranoia or hallucination of psychosis.

Over time, alcohol-triggered dopamine release can confuse our behaviour. We cannot but want rewards that are highlighted as important by dopamine. That is what it does in ordinary life. This means a bar or a bottle can seem for all the world like a pay check waiting to be cashed. The enjoyment we actually get from it, meanwhile, can become secondary.[97]

A dopamine-depleted rat does not ignore food because it is lazy. And it is not because it is stupid either, because rats in this condition still know the connection between food and a feeling of pleasure. Their apathy springs from an inability to give importance to the goal of eating. We might start to feel similarly listless after drinking too much.

We have far more complex and convoluted motivational challenges than rats, like doing our admin, housework, or the ironing. Such arduous tasks can become all the more difficult to do if alcohol has muddled our priorities. ■

# In the moment

Alcohol inebriation changes how we think, feel, and behave. The immediate effects are the same for the beer guzzler and wine connoisseur.

The most significant effect is that it reduces our brain activity, giving us a feeling of relaxation. Our mental horizons shrink, obscuring the significance of what is happening far away in time or distance. What matters to us is the here and now, while the rest is slowly consumed by mist. This narrowing of our horizons might mean we ignore an appointment the next day or even how to get home. The neural slowdown also manifests itself in increased "impulsivity", where we act with less consideration. Did I really just say that?

There is an exhilarating simplicity to making do with less brainpower too, like the thrill of speeding in an inadequate vehicle. Travelling at 20 miles-an-hour in a saloon car is boring but heart-pumping in a shopping trolley. Similarly, the mundane can become marvellous when our brains are configured to operate slowly. We also gain an effortless ability to focus on what is going on around us and look upon it with awe and amusement. "I drink to make other people interesting," said George Jean Nathan, an appropriately sniffy American New York drama critic in the first half of last century[98].

Our ideas become more fluid and susceptible to our surroundings in this state too, being more prone both to wild enthusiasm and heedless defeatism. We are more easily persuaded to back plans with a desirable goal with little concern for their feasibility.[99] But we are also more easily put off, ditching a plan more readily if its feasibility is queried. Once sober, we tend to return to a more consistent view again. So, fortunately, many drunken schemes do not become a reality.

But some aspects of the experience of inebriation stay with us, forming a parallel track in our thoughts. Memories formed under the influence of alcohol are split into a special class, being more easily remembered when we are inebriated again.[100] If we spend a lot of our time inebriated then stopping might mean we have restricted access to a large chunk of memories.

The chemically-blinkered state of inebriation described here has been given a name, "alcohol myopia".[101] While only a metaphor, it is a powerful one, offering a readily understandable characterisation of alcohol's immediate effects on behaviour, in all their strange diversity. Think of the short-sighted cartoon character Mr Magoo, and you are halfway there.

But even this simple picture throws up a mass of contradictions which it takes some extra effort to understand: Inebriation can make us more altruistic, but also more aggressive; It can relieve our anxiety and tension and yet underlie high drama and sudden crisis; It can make us feel that we are closer to how we would like to be, while also being able to leave us weeping over our inadequacies. People who have had a drink are more likely to disclose information about themselves, to gamble more, to be more gregarious and amorous, to the point of having more unprotected sex.

Smoking tobacco, meanwhile, appears to lower alcohol's myopic effect[102]. If you have an urge to smoke, however, alcohol will not help you resist it. Taken together these effects may partly explain why between 80 and 90 per cent of alcohol-dependent people smoke, three times the rate of the population as a whole.[103] The rate of alcohol dependency in smokers, meanwhile, is around ten times higher than among non-smokers. This is, perhaps, because of some genetic proclivity to alcohol and nicotine, like that of alcohol-preferring rodents.

Some of the myopic effects are the result of us acting out our expectations of what will happen after a drink or conforming to the behaviour expected of us. Similar behaviour changes are seen when we are given only placebo drinks. People who only think they have had a few drinks still tend to judge people's expressions to be happier than when they are sober and know it.[104]

But it is not all just make-believe because the effects of a drink are stronger. In extreme cases, for example, drunk people can function quite normally during a night out but are unable to recall what happened the following day.[105] No placebo has ever been recorded having this effect. Similarly, someone is unlikely to gamble away all their money, assault, or murder someone because they thought they had a drink. But these are well-documented behaviours of people who have had a real drink. Nor can alcohol be the only cause of behaviour changes while drunk, otherwise the same sort of thing would happen every time someone had a drink. The circumstances in which someone is inebriated plays a part too. The effects alcohol has on the brain are real, but the consequences depend on circumstances.

Alcohol intoxication has been found to compromise nearly every aspect of our information processing.[106] These including the ability to abstract and conceptualise, to encode large numbers of situational cues, to use several cues at the same time, and the use of active and systematic encoding strategies, which encodes meaning from incoming information and working memory.[107]

But this is more detail than we need to make sense of what is going on. Just two overriding impairments are enough to explain almost all drunken behaviour. The first of them is that alcohol intoxication consistently restricts the range of "cues" we notice, where these cues are the significant events around us or within our own being. And the second is that alcohol reduces the ability to process and extract meaning from the cues and information we do pick up.

"Like the bar mitzvah food in an old Woody Allen joke, the information we receive when we are drunk is bad and there isn't enough of it," as the 1990 paper which crystallised the idea of alcohol myopia put it. The drinker, it says, becomes "captive of an impoverished version of reality in which the breadth, depth, and timeline of understanding are constrained". This means poorly understood, immediate aspects of experience have a disproportionate influence on our behaviour and emotions.

Metaphorically speaking, we are like Mr Magoo bumping into trees, unable to see the forest around us. The keys to our actions when inebriated are the "salient" happenings in front of our noses. A drinker, for example, might respond to a provocation to have a fight, missing a security guard standing a few feet away. This reckless confrontation is the result of a restricted sphere of perception rather than bravado. "Dutch courage" is not a rise in a drinker's level of valour and bravery but a fall in their brain's capacity to see less obvious threats, like getting thrown out or prosecuted.[108]

Alcohol's brand of short-sightedness also leads us to adopt simplistic strategies which can lead to self-destructive aggression. In a 1979 laboratory experiment, intoxicated men were told they had been paired up with a partner who had the ability to send an unpleasant noise into their headphones. They were told they should respond as quickly as possible by turning a dial to give the person sending nasty noises an electric shock at a level of their choosing. The objective, they were told, was to bring an end to hostilities. The smart move to achieve this goal would be to send a very low-level shock in the hope it would be matched by an equally low-level noise from the other party.

In reality, it was not a human partner at the other end, but a computer which matched the level of electric shock with an equally nasty sound, according to an eye-for-an-eye principle. Sober subjects generally had the sense to work towards a low level of hostility. Intoxicated ones, however, tried to batter their way out of the conflict giving shocks three times the size, and paying the price by receiving tones on their headphones three times as nasty.

The difference in strategy is easily explained. For intoxicated participants, the "provocative" tone tended to be more salient than the idea that their aggression would elicit retaliation against them, which required a level of processing their intoxication prevented. So, they simply cranked up the retribution.

Other experiments have found that inebriated people are not only more aggressive than sober ones when faced with ambiguous provocations,[109] they are also more likely to miss indications that possible provocations are best ignored. In people with blood-alcohol concentrations of between 0.06 per cent and 0.14 per cent, a level typical of social drinking, intoxicated subjects were more extreme than 95 per cent of sober people. Fights are more common in societies where provocation and heavy drinking are common and less common where one ingredient is missing.

But alcohol myopia does not just lead to excessive aggression. Through a similar mechanism, it can make us more altruistic, sometimes excessively. If benevolence and kindness rather than aggression are the most salient cue in our sphere, we tend to be nicer when we are inebriated than when sober. Our kindness does not come from a profound sense of duty to our fellow man, but because our diminished processing power means we focus exclusively on cues to be helpful.

We might, for example, go to great lengths to help a stranger with a train ticket machine, only to miss our last train home. This is not an act of wilful self-sacrifice, but a case of acting on the cue that helping someone is the right thing to do without having the capacity to consider the consequences of doing so. Our inebriated bonhomie has few limits, so long as it remains the most salient cue in our environment. Experiments have also shown that drunk people give bigger tips and that all-male groups will tend to smile more at each other when they are inebriated.[110]

Whether for good or ill, there is little difference between the half-cut and the sober when there are no peripheral factors which conflict with the most immediate cue. But an inebriated person is likely to produce a very different reaction to a sober one when there is a cue which they miss. Our blindness to factors which might weigh against a response increases with the amount of alcohol we drink. The same goes for the ability to keep internal cues, or urges, in check as well as ones which are introduced from outside. Our excessive response to situations, therefore, rises too, depending on how much we have to drink.

Inebriation makes it hard, or even impossible, for us to learn tasks which require us to inhibit our inclinations. We are no different from rodents in this. Drunk rats were unable to learn tasks where success required them to inhibit their dominant tendencies. But when inhibition is not needed, drunken rats could learn just as well as sober ones. Tipsy humans too care less about making mistakes.[111] But we also make more bad decisions and make them more slowly.[112]

Alcohol skews our behaviour to fit with our immediate environment and inclinations. Whether this is beneficial is a lottery. Lowering our inhibition can help if our goal is to perform karaoke, but it is also the mechanism which stops us from stepping off the curb into the path of a passing bus.

Alcohol myopia has a similar effect on our internal life as it does on our view of the world around us. Most of us tend to think of ourselves as fine and admirable people, so when inebriated we tend to miss outlying thoughts to moderate this self-regard, which can lead us to grandiosity and boastfulness.

Irritating as it may be, big-headedness is perhaps the most benign of its effects. It also tends to accentuate other tendencies. People who have a tendency to be mean, sentimental, fearful, quick to stereotype, self-criticise, or consider suicide, might find alcohol puts their personal preoccupation centre stage.[113] People who get aggressive when they are drunk tend to be angrier to begin with.[114] This is one case in which *in vino veritas*, or alcohol as a truth serum, has some backing. Alcohol drinking can sometimes mean we act out a simplified version of ourselves. Is it fair, however, to judge someone who is temporarily disabled, albeit by their own hand?

Another notable effect of alcohol myopia is that we tend to drink more.[115] Inebriated drinkers are surrounded by social cues like other people drinking. In a bar, we will also be targeted by eye-catching marketing saying, in essence, "Another drink is a really, really good idea." The mental myopia means we may miss contrary messages saying, "Another drink is definitely a bad idea." This means a "quick drink" can often turn into a protracted session. It is not spontaneous fun which consumes us. Instead, alternatives simply disappear from our awareness.

Impulsivity, a symptom of alcohol myopia, has a glamour to it. Scores of medals are awarded to men and women who acted impulsively, often doing things which defy self-interest. In civvy street a glint of impulsivity has a wow factor too. An impulsive action with an amusing or positive outcome might be seen as daring, spontaneous, creative, or brave. This potential for generating lucky flukes might help give alcohol a special allure for men, particularly young ones, looking to boost their devil-may-care image.

A series of UK television ads for a women's deodorant in the 80s and early 90s, called "Impulse", captured the romantic idea of impulsivity well. Typically, a man would be innocently walking down the street when he would get a whiff of a woman who had sprayed herself with the deodorant. Then, possessed by desire, the impulsive man would sprint to the nearest florist, buy a bunch of flowers, and present them to the modestly astonished woman. The strapline would then appear on screen, "Men can't help acting on Impulse." Such behaviour might come under the definition of harassment these days. Nevertheless, acting on the spur of the moment is still considered an attractive attribute, speaking of raw passion, and someone who sometimes allows their heart to rule their head. Never mind that nobody's actions are ever dictated by their heart. An impulsive person is someone ready to defy petty convention and consequences to satisfy their deepest urges. Alcohol, as we have seen, can definitely help with this.

The consequences of impulsivity beyond the confines of an old TV advertisement can be less satisfactory. Impulsive actions can be seen as stupid, dangerous or, in extreme cases, immoral or criminal. And there is generally no special consideration for people who did something impulsively criminal while inebriated. Around 40 per cent of violent crimes are committed while drunk and around the same percentage of people in US jails say they were drunk when they were arrested.[116]

This is an unfortunate cycle: with social pressure to be impulsive; alcohol boosting impulsivity; and impulsivity boosting social problems. Measures of impulsivity, meanwhile, have been shown to be related to our ability to control alcohol intake. People who get a high score on a measure called the Barratt Impulsivity Scale (BIS) tend to find it more difficult to resist having another drink, which in turn will increase their impulsivity.

Alcohol myopia undermines drinkers' risk assessments related to sex too. Inebriated students said they would be more willing to have unprotected sex with a hypothetical new partner shown to them in a video.[117] The decision was unchanged by indications made in the film that the hypothetical partner had many previous partners, making them higher risks for contracting sexually transmitted diseases. The only effect of this was to reduce the number of people who said they consider the interviewee for girlfriend or boyfriend. This is a curiously inconsistent mix of short-termism and, seemingly, long-term thinking.

The biggest factor in this risk taking seems to be a drinker's brain power, or "cognitive reserve", rather than their sex drive.[118] Those with lower abilities in reading, arithmetic, and spelling were more likely to say they would have unprotected sex with the person in the video. A mediaeval idea of a truly romantic heart ruling someone's head may underlie a drinking culture which creates a virtue out of a cognitive problem and a cognitive problem into a social one.

Alcohol has also been shown to give drinkers a more sympathetic eye for other people's appearance, a phenomenon known in drinking circles as "beer goggles". More rigorous investigation has confirmed the finding. A group of 84 men and women were given either alcohol or a placebo to drink and asked to score photos of male and female faces for attractiveness.[119] And the findings confirmed pub lore: those who drank alcohol found the faces more attractive, regardless of the gender of the drinker. One gender difference did appear, with male participants who drank alcohol continuing to rate female faces more highly a day after. The experimenters put the effect down to a shift in aesthetic standards. The effect is not limited to rating other people's appearance either. Another study found a drink made people judge landscapes at the lower end of the scale as more attractive.[120]

Away from sexual hurly-burly, we find that alcohol myopia can help us chill out and be free from doubts and worries. The positive mind-numbing effects can be improved if we occupy our attention with some simple activity. Watching football or playing a bar game while slightly sozzled can be more absorbing than usual, so distracting us from our niggling worries. Eating is also enhanced, with the senses—particularly smell—sharpened.[121] To get the same effect of quieting the inner babble without inebriation, you might need to play sport, play a game, play a musical instrument, read, meditate, or draw.

While inebriation can enhance our appreciation of the moment, it is no great concentration-enhancer. Inebriated people spend about a quarter of the time with their minds wandering from what they are doing, about twice as much as sober people.[122] But, despite zoning-out for one out of every five minutes, they notice drifting away half as often as sober people. Inebriated people, then, are unreliable witnesses of their own attention. So, while it may be relaxing, being tiddly can mean missing a fifth of our free time and missing our more imaginative thoughts.

There are several attempts to explain impulsivity, which is the engine of alcohol's attraction and of its problems. One is that of cognitive depletion—sometimes called more dramatically "ego depletion"—where our ability to bring our behaviour into line with our goals, ideals, values, morals, and social expectations is curtailed. This is based on the observation that the brain has a limited capacity to override one response to make another one possible.

In old moralistic parlance, this limitation might be looked at as "giving into temptation". Depletion theory, which has no moral overtones, proposes a similar mechanism minus agents of the devil, by saying we all have a limited "reservoir" of self-control which, when depleted, results in a reduced capacity for self-regulation. Just as our muscles get tired, so does our ability to control our behaviour. This is what researchers call the "cognitive depletion of self-control". Resisting different things all seem to sap the same reservoir of self-control. So, resisting the urge to check our Facebook account or eating the chocolate bar in the desk drawer could mean it later seems impossible for us to stick to our shopping budget.

That is not to say that it makes sense to simply hide from temptations, however. There is evidence that you can enlarge your self-control muscle by exercising it. And, also, successfully controlling behaviour in one area can help you control behaviour in others. It seems that stretching our cognitive reserve without overstretching, may help us slow our rate of cognitive depletion. The "character-forming" activities dished out at school, like football practice in a hail storm, may serve some purpose, as a kind of self-control training.

Everyone has a limit, however. No matter how highly-trained our self-control is, we can still hit a point where there is nothing left. For someone who wants to drink, it is a double peril: resisting alcohol places an extra burden on the mechanisms of self-control while giving into it will undermine the mechanism both in breaking the self-control and because of alcohol's tendency to increase impulsivity.

Self-control and the loss of it create paradoxes. A decision to limit or stop drinking alcohol can itself be made impulsively, although carrying it out successfully requires self-control. Hence, "never-again-syndrome" when we resolve to stop drinking the day after a heavy night, only to break it almost immediately. And self-control also is not the antithesis of spontaneity, because it allows us to act without being unduly influenced by our worries and immediate surroundings.

Drinking offers us a sense of freedom from our everyday thoughts and feelings. We can enter a world where the moment matters most, and we are immersed in it. This has much to recommend it as a way to spend our spare moments. We can spend too long ignoring the pleasures of the here-and-now. But there is nothing very pleasurable about alcohol inebriation when it goes wrong. There is only so much we can expect from disabling our brains. ■

# Groupdrink

Heavy drinking, with all its warm, carefree bonhomie, is among the habits which help bring people together. It is, perhaps, unsurprising it could be seen as an activity which defines a nation. An appreciation of alcohol effortlessly crosses political and social divisions, being a shared quirk of our digestion and nervous systems.

The downside can be something like what George Orwell called "groupthink" in his dystopian novel *1984*. To pick one example out of many, a nominally liberal British paper called *The Independent* published a news story about how a half of a group of people who tried to give up drinking in January 2015 had not managed it.[123] It described the struggling teetotallers as "smug dry braggers". The justification for the barbed description was, apparently, the people in question had told their acquaintances they were going to try to have a "dry January" on Facebook. It may be a little unwise sometimes to share personal goals like this, but it is even more foolish for a national newspaper to accuse people they have not interviewed of being "smug". It would, surely, be more consistent for a paper that espouses liberal values to ask why so many young people were unable to follow through with their decision to lay-off alcohol drinking? This is surely more appropriate than using column inches to glory in their failure.

This is not a one-off. People who stop drinking are often called "smug". It is a tricky accusation to deny, as is any presumption of our thoughts or motivations. It is a variant on, "I know what you are thinking, and I do not like it." Too forceful a denial could be taken to validate the apparently damning charge of being happy with a decision you have made. It is all the more confusing because the term "smug" suggests the person using it also thinks a decision is a good one, only having a problem with someone else going through with it. Is it really wrong to be happy to pursue a good decision? And isn't it extremely mean-spirited to insult others for doing as they please with their lives? The reason for picking on abstainers seems more likely to be an attempt to prevent a perceived betrayal of a dominant group. But the question is, who is betraying who? The person who does what they think is right for them at no cost to anyone else or the person who insults them for it?

What is the reason for the peevish reception of newly-minted abstainers as betrayers to a cause-as-yet-unknown? It might be the belief that people abstain competitively or narcissistically, rather than to improve their lives. Or, perhaps, abstainers are suspected attempting to shame others for their drinking? That could be it. All in all, it is perhaps better not to invite unkind speculation about our motives by "going public", particularly in a competitive social environment like Facebook. But attempting to keep quitting quiet is no guarantee of peace either. People feel quite entitled to "out" an abstainer, perhaps labelling them a fanatic, quite possibly thinking they are "smug" for not mentioning it. Sadly, there is no perfect solution.

As a finale, the piece on the "smug" abstainers goes on to describe those who have not achieved their goal of a dry January as having "fallen off the wagon". This image harks back to people being swept up by religiously-motivated temperance movements in the nineteenth century. It is an amusing image to think of, no doubt: Credulous people being swept up to do something in religious fervour. Haha. The problem with the image is, however, that it portrays the current situation the wrong way round. Few now stop drinking for religious reasons, having plenty of science and medicine to back up their choice, while the decision to continue drinking heavily relies on blind faith.

The strange effect of this topsy-turvy situation in which unreason is given the whip hand is that we can feel they have to go from being outgoing heavy drinkers to bashful non-drinker. We can find it harder to be outgoing if they are not inebriated, of course. But it seems likely that some of the changes in our social behaviour can be attributed to the wish to avoid casual insults.

Despite such downsides, large numbers of us successfully go from dependence to moderate drinking or abstinence. It is simply unreasonable to pick on someone for the contents of their glass.

Alcohol has found a privileged niche in politics too. Its consumption is for many an expression of our personal freedom, a minor act of rebellion. It is quite understandable to think this, given the unruly behaviour which can result and the dwindling number of risks and thrills we are exposed to. But it is ironic that it is considered a minor triumph of liberty to consume a highly-taxed drug that saps the mental resources we need to enjoy our autonomy.

There seems no shifting the idea of alcohol as a liquid liberator. But, in reality, restricting our alcohol consumption is not giving in to conformity or convention. Abstaining is, looked at more plainly, a move away from conformity in most western societies where drinking is the norm. Not drinking also tends to improve our abilities to make plans and carry them out, so making ourselves freer to act as we wish. Is that not liberty? If we act unusually when we are drunk, by contrast, it is because our outlook is obscured and options limited. The same choices are still available to us when we are sober, and often many more.

Our own decision to consume alcohol should not be pushed on anyone else. America's experiment with alcohol prohibition went spectacularly awry despite having some upsides. Informally enforcing drinking is no more likely to succeed. Instead, we need to be allowed to make our own informed choices.

Governments can do their part by restricting advertising containing misleading imagery and by requiring clear warnings on alcohol products. And we can inform ourselves and our children. And we can make it easier for people by respecting their decision to cut down or abstain. ■

# And so to bed

Just as the working brain is a mystery, so is its downtime, sleep. Without it, our nervous system would go haywire, closely followed by the body it regulates. Alcohol has been found to disrupt the sleeping process while being widely used to help us drop off.

As we know from our dreams, the sleeping brain is not simply turned off during sleep. But being a solitary, inactive, internalised state, it is difficult to penetrate. From the outside, you can measure brain activity using non-invasive imaging techniques or by measuring electromagnetic activity using sensors on the scalp. From these readings, the functions of different phases of sleep, where the activity patterns are different, are deduced from the difficulties people or animals have if they are deprived of them.

It seems, in essence, that sleep's function is to repair and clean the brain's mental hardware and consolidate the learning of the previous day. To do so, it cycles through sleep of four types. There is some ambiguity and overlap between them, but each is typified by signature waves and sharp peaks of neuronal activity. We tend to have difficulty with different mental activities when denied sleep of each kind.

The first of the four phases is a dozing state, known as "N1," when our body becomes limp and sometimes twitches as we lose awareness of our surroundings. In this stage, our cerebral cortex has entered into light hibernation. The frequency of the waves of brain activity halve, measured using electrodes on the scalp. Undisturbed, we will then slip into an intermediate phase of sleep called, rather predictably, "N2". In this state, we become completely cut off from the environment around us. We typically spend around half our sleep time in this N2 state. In this state, unlike N1, our brain activity is punctuated by spikes and bursts, called "K-complexes" and "spindles", which appear to help keep us unconscious.

Then there is N3 sleep, a form of deep sleep. During this the underlying rhythm of brain waves is at its strongest and slowest, having peaks and troughs with half or even a quarter of the frequency of that seen in N1. These low, deep rhythms need only be seen for a fifth of the time for sleep to be logged as N3, but the proportion can be twice this. Blood flow in the cerebral cortex, the part of the brain which does the thinking, is typically 25 per cent lower than when we are awake. When we are woken from N3, with our cortexes on standby, we tend to feel groggy and find mental tasks difficult.

N3 seems to be when some key functions of the cerebral cortex are restored. Deprived of N3 sleep we still function well physically but can have trouble concentrating and, in extreme cases, can experience hallucinations. If we are deprived of N3, we also have trouble forming factual memories, while being artificially induced to have more N3 has been shown to give us better factual memories.[124] The relative importance of N3 to someone's survival is suggested by it being given the highest priority when we are "catching up" on sleep.[125]

Then for the most mysterious of the four types of sleep, typically accounting for about a quarter of our sleep time, rapid eye movement (REM) sleep. For this our motor neurotransmitters are turned off, paralysing our bodies. Our body is paralysed, that is, apart from our genitals which are, unaccountably, turned on. The brain waves speed up again, and the eyes roll about, hence the name, not even always pointing in the same direction. This seems to be where our dreams are made because we will often be able to recall dreams if we are woken up during it.

Animals and people whose bodies are not paralysed during REM will act out their dreams. Cats will stalk and pounce as if they were hunting. This might tie in with REM's proposed function of laying down memories of physical and mental skills, as opposed to the storing of factual knowledge in N2. Others contest this, however. Another curious observation is that people who are depressed will often find they can feel better for having less REM. This effect can be seen in normal life when people on a downer are markedly more cheerful after being woken up earlier than normal. Some speculate that, in excess, REM can become draining rather than restoring.

It is easy enough to observe how alcohol can help people initiate the sleeping process, inducing N1 sleep. Taking a late train on a Friday night is enough to suggest its efficiency. Science confirms the observation too, although no-one knows exactly how it does it, although its effect of reducing brain activity is doubtless part of it. But alcohol does not just kickstart the sleeping process, it changes other aspects of sleep which only more detailed monitoring can uncover. The disruption seems to be greater in women.[126]

Observation of inebriated sleepers shows that alcohol delays the first period of REM sleep, reducing the proportion of REM sleep in the first half of the night in adults. In the second half of sleep, however, as blood-alcohol levels drop and some degree of hangover begins, the proportion of REM sleep increases, but not enough to compensate for the loss in the first half.[127] It seems not to change the proportions of REM and non-REM sleep in adolescents, however.[128] The effect on REM sleep seems to change if it is taken on two successive evenings too.[129] Mice fell to sleep more easily and got more non-REM shuteye on the first day they were inebriated, but not after a second day on the sauce.

Alcohol's effect on sleep quality is more complicated still if you consider the nature of the sleep phases as well as their proportions. Alcohol appears to deepen the delta-waves associated with the N3 stage of deep sleep, where the cortex is supposed to be powered-down.[130] But, in adolescents, alcohol has also been found to create disturbances, with an increase in frontal "alpha waves" a pattern not normal in sleep.[131] Alpha brain waves are generally linked to wakeful relaxation with the eyes closed.

This cocktail of "alpha-delta" sleep is also often seen in people with depression and conditions involving chronic fatigue, like fibromyalgia or rheumatoid arthritis.[132] People with these medical conditions commonly complain of not feeling fully refreshed by their night's sleep, as do some people who have been drinking heavily.

The brain is not the only part of the central nervous system that alcohol affects. Alcohol also disturbs a basic part of the nervous system controlling unconscious actions, called the autonomic nervous system.[133] The autonomic functions it controls include breathing, heart regulation, and certain reflex actions such as coughing, sneezing, swallowing, and vomiting. It is divided into two parts: one part, called the "sympathetic", is in charge of active responses and another, called the "parasympathetic", is in charge of resting and recovering. Together they perform a kind of nervous balancing act: when one is active, the other tends to be less so, a relative state which can be measured by analysing the variability of heart rate. Measuring the autonomic nerve system of inebriated people suggests that our autonomic nervous system, metaphorically speaking, lies awake when we sleep inebriated. The balance of the autonomic nervous system is on the active side rather than the resting one. This suggests that our nervous systems and bodies might not be getting as much rest if we sleep under the influence.

An alcohol binge, meanwhile, seemingly disturbs the internal clock which tells us if it is time to be awake or asleep. Researchers injected rats with alcohol during their wakeful period, simulating a typical human binge.[134] They slept normally the next time bedtime came round, but the following sleep time they became insomniacs. Having slept less during this normal sleep time, they caught up with catnaps during their next active period. Only on the third day after their involuntary binge did their sleep patterns start to return to normal. A similar study showed rats of the strain that has a taste for alcohol have, by some cruel stroke of luck, their sleep pattern more thrown-off by a period of simulated binging than normal rats.[135] These same booze-oriented rats also suffered a period of insomnia in the days that followed.

Wholesale binging is not necessarily the only way alcohol might mess up the body's clockwork either. Moderate drinking also seems to be able to throw sleep off-kilter. Drinking regular, moderate amounts, like a glass of wine with dinner every day, in the kind of amounts that are said to have cardiovascular benefits, was found to be enough to disrupt the human internal clock and slow reactions.[136] The reduction in the amount and quality of REM sleep provoked by moderate amounts of alcohol may also mean it is harder for us to remember how to solve puzzles.[137] Our attention spans too also seem to be reduced.[138]

There is still only a sketch of what effect alcohol may have on the sleeping brain. But, in most people, it appears to reduce the quantity and quality of sleep, with a troubling connection to provoking the mysterious "alpha-delta" sleep, an intrusion of wakeful brain patterns into sleep time that is linked to depression and fatigue. At the same time, it seems the autonomic immune system appears to be shifted towards an active rather than resting state.

If we drink enough to develop a dependency, we can find that our sleep continues to be disturbed after giving up. Those of us who have at some point been dependent on alcohol often get less than the normal amount of slow wave sleep even two years after we stop drinking. Taking a "drop to help you sleep" is a dose of bad medicine. ■

# The morning after

The hangover is part-and-parcel of life for many of us, with stoical forbearance being the only mature and civilised response. The preventative strategy of not drinking has been proved one hundred per cent effective, while an effective remedy which allows us to drink is as elusive as the philosopher's stone.

The hangover's medical nickname, *veisalgia*, was a recent creation. It is bolted together from the Viking word *kveis*, meaning a feeling of post-coital sadness, and *algia*, the Greek for pain. Its double dose of unpleasantness is suggestive of just how crummy hangovers can still make would-be Viking marauders feel after one or two horns too many.

The feeling of post-coital sadness is, perhaps, restricted to humans, but our animal brethren share many more quantifiable *veisalgia* symptoms. Hungover mice are weaker, less inquisitive, and more agitated and fearful while suffering deficits in their reward systems.[139,140,141] And, just as the severity of hangovers we experience varies from one person to the next, members of other species have different levels of hangover depending on their genetic background.

Experiments on variants of the much-studied *C elegans* roundworm, for instance, showed that British varieties suffer worse hangovers than Hawaiian ones.[142] It is not, apparently, that British *C elegans* are simply making a fuss.

In fact, British often downplay the ill-effects of a bender, a cornerstone of the island social life, to that of a "sore head". It would not do to make a drama out of a crisis, particularly one which is manifestly self-inflicted. Many come to regard a hangover as a price levied for a good time or, as the case may be, a fitting punishment for straying from the straight and narrow. In some circles, the haggard expression of a hangover is cause for amusement born of a woozy cocktail of empathy and schadenfreude. So, although retribution is not meted out fairly, the overriding ethos is to take a painkiller and carry on, perhaps acknowledging one's culpability for good measure. One might add to this a simmering resentment for anyone not suffering the same fate.

This stoicism is admirable in many ways and is also warranted since hangovers tend to feel worse than their measurable effects. But anyone who has had a severe hangover knows the misery to be far more all-embracing than a "sore head" which is often only the tiny tip of an enormous iceberg of unpleasantness. Common hangover symptoms include drowsiness, problems concentrating, dry mouth, dizziness, upset stomach, sweating, nausea, hyper-excitability, heart pounding, shivering, clumsiness, anxiety, confusion, fear, low mood, emotional disturbance, and a general feeling of being unwell.[143]  All of these symptoms can last for 24 hours or more. So diverse are they that researchers have devised ways to calibrate the misery on a 12-point scale, bringing together 47 different symptoms[144]. Greater understanding of the subtleties of the phenomenon now may be at hand with the founding, in 2010, of the Alcohol Hangover Research Group.[145]

Such grim aftereffects would normally be enough to deter people from engaging in an activity. But few of us stop after our first warning. Most of our attempts to learn from the shocking experience turn out to be manifestations of never again syndrome, where resolution is forgotten once the hangover is gone. Around three-quarters of Americans who have consumed intoxicating doses of alcohol have experienced a hangover and around 15 per cent of people will have had a hangover in the last month.[146] Other figures suggest that half of the people who consume one or two drinks per day have experienced a hangover in the previous year. Around 40 per cent of heavy drinkers, meanwhile, say they have had a hangover at least once a month, while only a quarter of alcoholic patients complain of them.

Like most mechanisms involved in alcohol consumption, hangovers are messy and do not reveal their secrets lightly. Many variables have been identified which contribute to their severity, but none is dominant. Our genetic makeup is thought to account for around 45 per cent of the variance.[147] So, as a punitive measure for foolishness, it is extremely unfair, punishing some more than others simply because of our family backgrounds.

The lack of a definite cause even includes the level of inebriation. Blood-alcohol concentration is a factor in the severity of a hangover, with a peak blood-alcohol concentration of 0.10 per cent—about three or four drinks—needed to provoke a hangover in most of us, but some people may only need half that concentration.[148] Then there are those of us who get off very lightly. Around a quarter of people can reach blood-alcohol concentrations of 0.10 per cent and higher and have no hangover to speak of.

Hangover, the effect of withdrawal from short-term exposure to alcohol, can hit the new drinker as hard as the grizzled barfly. Withdrawal symptoms, however, are the result of long-term exposure that causes brain adaptations which prolong post-binge suffering. The lines between the two can often blur. Generally, acute withdrawal symptoms start later, not the morning after a session, and could go on for several days. Hangovers, by contrast, tend to start a few hours after and disappear after 24 hours. Some sleep disturbance from a hangover may linger on, however.

If we are alcohol dependent, then, we can experience a nasty double-whammy after a session, with a hangover merging into withdrawal effects. Some alcohol-dependent people, however, follow a different pattern and proceed straight to withdrawal symptoms without first passing through a hangover. A fundamental difference is that the central nervous system of someone with a hangover is generally slowed, while that of an alcohol-dependent person in withdrawal is hyper-excitable.

At their most extreme, the extra discomforts awaiting the dependent drinker include seizures, severe agitated confusion—known in the trade as *delirium tremens*—and sometimes we can have hallucinations. In serious cases, these acute withdrawal symptoms can require hospitalisation and the administration of sedatives and anticonvulsants.[149] Most dependent drinkers, however, have far less dramatic withdrawal symptoms, like sweating, anxiety, and nausea.

There are some potentially misleading similarities between hangover and withdrawal. Both hangovers and withdrawal symptoms can be temporarily eased by having an alcoholic drink. This kind of "relief drinking" may provide one route by which heavy drinkers start drinking with the regularity needed to become dependent. This may explain the counterintuitive finding that people who suffer the worst hangovers are more likely to become dependent.[150] By drinking to escape their nasty hangovers, they smooth the path to the brain adaptations of dependency.

In a confusion typical of the subject, other studies have shown that the severity of someone's alcohol hangovers can also have the more rational response of curbing appetite for alcohol. What seems fairly clear, however, is that regular hangovers mean someone is drinking at a level which is having an impact on their brain and nervous system. To continue could mean the brain tries to adapt to cope with it.

It would seem clear from casual observation that people with hangovers are not in good mental shape. Drowsiness and poor cognitive functioning are the most common complaints.[151] Nevertheless, these seemingly debilitating problems have not easily succumbed to measurement.[152] This is partly because of the limitations of what experiments can measure, but it is also reasonable to say that hangovers feel considerably worse than they actually are.

That's not to say there is no effect at all. Several lab experiments have shown that our ability to maintain attention falls during hangover.[153] Hungover people are also slower when asked to concentrate and click when they see a certain letter appear on a screen. They are also less on-the-ball, having trouble responding quickly to an image that might appear anywhere on a screen while tracking a target with a joystick.

These reductions in performance have obvious implications for would-be drivers. Hungover people have also been found to weave more and lose their concentration more on a driving simulator when hungover.[154] In one study, drivers with impaired driving skills who were not high or drunk had far more elevated readings of ethyl glucuronide and ethyl sulfate in their blood, both suggesting they were driving on a hangover.[155] And, in another test, the overhung were found to be more easily distracted and also perform worse than normal in the Stroop Task, where the subject needs to identify the colour used to write the word for a different colour. The challenge is suppressing the urge to say the written word rather than identify the colour it is written in.

Rigorous laboratory experiments have, however, been less dramatic than might be imagined by those with a damp flannel cooling their brow. It could be partly be because people overestimate the level of impairment. But it could also be that lab experiments do not reproduce the way we drink in real life. The pace of drinking and other factors, like food consumption or going to sleep late, might all change the outcome. And non-lab tests, which observe drinkers in their natural habitat, which measure the performance of people before and after a night's drinking do not include a placebo trial. This lack of placebo means there is a chance that that people taking part in these experiments may have performed as badly as they did because they expected to be groggy, not because they were genuinely impaired.

But, still, there is some consistency in the cognitive effects shown across the laboratory, as well as studies of drinkers in the wild, which show hangover-related memory and attention problems.[156] It seems likely then that our performance at work when we are hungover also suffers. And it is also reasonable to assume that the effects of hangovers significantly reduce our capacity to fulfil commitments in our private lives.

While the price of a hangover seems to be becoming clearer, the cause is still uncertain. The bulk of hangover research goes back to the 70s with experiments often only done on small groups of men, who most likely have a different reaction than women.[157]

Some factors can be ruled out. Blood and urine samples show concentrations of various hormones, electrolytes, free fatty acids, triglycerides, lactate, ketone bodies, cortisol, and glucose were not significantly related to hangover severity. Also, markers of dehydration, which is widely rumoured to be the main reason we feel lousy, was not connected to hangover severity either.

There seem to be other contributing factors too. Some studies show a significant correlation between hangover severity and the concentration of acetaldehyde, a toxic chemical which forms part-way through the digestion of alcohol. But, while raised acetaldehyde seems to worsen hangovers, it seems not to be the driving force either. In white people, it tends to be at low concentration during hangover compared to East Asians, who can sometimes not digest acetaldehyde as efficiently. It could still be, though, that acetaldehyde causes problems during the drinking phase and the hangover represents a rebalancing of the system after the fact. More research is being done to find out.

Other factors which do not cause alcohol hangover but can increase its severity are sleep deprivation, cigarette smoking, and a drinker's health status and, of course, their genetics.[158] Chemicals called "congeners", the by-products of fermentation, may make hangovers worse too, with congener-heavy bourbon being more liable to cause a nasty hangover than more rarefied vodka. Minute concentrations of methanol, one congener, ethanol's toxic little brother, can hang around in the body for ten hours after drinking. But again, it cannot be the main culprit, because people also suffer hangovers after drinking absolutely pure ethanol. Other congeners like isopentanol, ethylic acetate, and ethyl formate, may also be aggravating factors.[159]

A recent experiment found differences in the metabolism of the brains of hungover mice.[160] Confirming this would require further investigation, however. There have also been studies showing that hangover severity may be reduced using drugs which reduce the synthesis of "prostaglandins", compounds spread widely around the body that have signalling functions similar to hormones.

The main chemicals present in alcoholic drinks and their digestion have all been eliminated as the overriding cause of hangovers. They play bit parts, but not the leading role. This has led some to the conclusion that the cause might be traced to the body's response rather than to the chemicals themselves.

This hypothesis argues that all these different factors might contribute to a response from the body's defence system. This would mean our hangover symptoms result from a triggering of our inflammatory response to perceived chemical invaders. It could be this response which causes symptoms like nausea, headache, and fatigue not the invaders. A possible remedy might then be to reduce the immune response, using "cyclooxygenase inhibitors" like aspirin, ibuprofen, and a variety of naturally occurring ones like fish oils.

It could be that alcohol's effect of disrupting recovery of the autonomic nerve system—which controls our "automatic", lower level bodily functions—can also shed light on drinking's mysterious aftereffects.[161] Staying in a darkened room may help reset the body clock if someone has the luxury of doing so without disturbance, but its effectiveness has only so far been scientifically shown in a study of Swiss mice.[162]

The discomfort of a hangover is, surely, a warning sign that the body is being thrown off balance. This is true no matter how stoically we endure them. If we suffered the same ill-effects after practically any other activity, we would stop. Yet we choose to endure them repeatedly, sometimes regularly. This enormous degree of forgiveness is a testament to alcohol's beguiling charm and the apparently nonsensical special pleading we give it.

Hangovers are not symptoms of dependence themselves, but the willingness to endure them means the door to developing dependence is wide open. Drinking enough to provoke hangovers over a long period may be all we need to do. Initially, withdrawal symptoms may be masked by the hangover too, appearing as some mysterious unpleasant appendix. The "two-day hangovers" we sometimes talk about do not exist. Suffering significantly after 24 hours is likely to be a sign of some degree of dependence.

As with the common cold, there is no cure for the common hangover. Given the millions who suffer them, this is a major gap in scientific discovery. There is, however, a one hundred per cent sure-fire preventative treatment, which is not drinking much. The only problem with it is implementation. "Hardened" drinkers, meanwhile, unwilling to change their habits, will have to wait for an unexpected breakthrough. If the immune system is to blame for our *veisalgia*, it could be a long wait. ∎

# Downing drinks

Alcohol not only blunts our ability to think on the hoof, but it also alters the way we feel. Regular drinking can destabilise our mood, fuelling depression and anxiety.

It is implicated in a vast number of cases. Nobody can be sure about exactly how many it involved because cause and effect are difficult to apply to the complex whirl of our mental activity. One indication of the scale of the association, however, is that people who drink heavily are more than twice as likely to suffer from depression and anxiety as moderate drinkers.[163] And as many as a third of debilitating "major depressions" may be attributable to alcohol dependence. People are coy about admitting to mental health problems, but the US government reckons around 14 per cent of Americans suffer from some kind of mental illness, with depression and anxiety the most common of them. There is little understanding of the connection with alcohol. Laddish advice on the subject might be for someone to "grow a pair" and get a round in.

The medical establishment is in a muddle. "Alcohol consumption is associated with many other neuropsychiatric conditions, such as depression or anxiety disorder, but the complexity of the pathways of these associations currently prevents their inclusion in the estimates of alcohol-attributable disease burden," says the World Health Organisation (WHO), the UN's health wing in its 2014 report on alcohol and health.[164] A decade earlier, the same organisation published an expert assessment which concluded there was indeed a causal link, saying, "Overall, we find sufficient evidence of causality for the influence of alcohol dependence on depressive disorders. The evidence indicates that a clear and consistent association exists between alcohol dependence and depressive disorders and that chance, confounding variables, and other bias can be ruled out with reasonable confidence as factors in this association."

So that is as clear as mud. For the sake of clarity, then, let us focus on the bilateral connection rather than on strict causality. Depression tends to happen more to us when on an alcoholic bender. Around a third of severe depressive episodes suffered by men with alcohol problems only happened when they were drinking heavily, according to a 30-year study of 400 men.[165] Stopping drinking, or cutting down, meanwhile, has been found to relieve depression and anxiety. Drinking may not have been the initial cause of our blues, but not drinking has been found to be highly likely to provide relief within weeks or even just a few days.[166] Depression can make it more likely we drink too, so the risk reinforcement circle is complete. The same study also found that people who had severe depression were at more risk of developing alcohol problems.

The more alcohol we consumed, the more symptoms of depression we are likely to experience.[167] A quarter of alcohol-dependent Americans suffered major depression in the last year, and a similar number had some kind of problem with anxiety.[168] And around 16 per cent of people who are depressed also have an alcohol use problem, mainly to the level of dependence, and around 13 per cent of people with anxiety also have an alcohol issue, again mostly that of dependence.

Heavy drinking and less severe depression seem almost certain to fuel each other too, although the connection is even more difficult to discern. The lack of hard data does not mean there is no connection, however. It may simply lie beyond the limits of statistics.

The difficulty in proving a causal relationship between drinking and depression and anxiety is a nuisance to scientists and leaves a gaping hole in public awareness. You can never be sure if your depression is caused by alcohol use or it is the other way round. Are we gloomy because we drink or drinking because we are gloomy, or "self-medicating" in the jargon? Solving this riddle once and for all would have serious implications, moral and legal, for both consumers and alcohol producers.

Doing so will be a challenge. But the quest to establish a cause and effect relationship between depression and alcohol may be like finding whether chickens cause eggs or the other way round. The interdependence between them is enough to take effective action if your aim is to reduce the chicken or egg population. Remove the eggs, and there will be fewer chickens.

Just to add to the downer alcohol offers us, around two-thirds of alcohol-dependent men suffer some form of sexual dysfunction, no great lift to the spirits. Around two-thirds of those with sexual dysfunction lack sexual desire, while many have trouble gaining or maintaining an erection and a small number have problems with premature ejaculation. This may be connected to alcohol's interference with the reward system of people's brains or the autonomic nervous system which plays a part in arousal. The good news is that these difficulties also tend to go away if people lay off the drink, assuming there are no physical problems.[169]

Drinking large quantities of alcohol also, as outlined in the last chapter, compromises the ability to access useful information and make quick decisions. This means that when we push the alcohol limits, we are more likely to make more blunders, which is also likely to lower our spirits. Heavy drinkers are, therefore, more likely to be hit with a traumatic event and less able to deal with one. They are also more likely than most to seek solace in alcohol. Psychological pressures like divorce or a job loss, or accidents, childhood mistreatment, and the chronic stress of being part of a minority can all increase drinking.[170]

Many people probably know to some level that alcohol is a depressant, but do not act accordingly. The baffling problem of cause-and-effect distracts our attention. So too does the fact that depression often has a rational basis. And, mental health, with us being bound up in our self-respect and respect for others, remains a touchy subject. The alcohol industry is keen to muddy the issue where it can.

Drink Aware, the UK's alcohol-industry-backed public health initiative, does acknowledge that there is some connection. "If you drink heavily and regularly, you're likely to develop some symptoms of depression."[171] But the words "likely" and "some symptoms of depression", rather than real depression, massively water down the message. And the page also keeps the door slightly ajar to the idea that drinking might actually be a stress reliever, by saying "a glass of wine after a hard day might help you relax...". It would be more accurate to say: you might think a glass of wine helps you relax, but the findings strongly suggest you are wrong. In more plain language, drinking to relieve stress or anxiety is counter-productive, and heavy drinkers are at risk of developing depression.

This kind of token acknowledgement of alcohol's mental health impact is woefully inadequate to address the problem. By the time someone has unearthed the Alcohol Aware website, it is more than likely too late anyway. Our habits and alcohol expectancies will already be so deeply ingrained that one line is unlikely to inspire the wholesale rethink we need, assuming we ever find it. To have any real effect, the message cannot be left in the wilderness. It needs to be printed on every drink sold, leaving out the word "cause", if need be. The warning can read, "Heavy drinkers are depressed more often."

It is, doubtless, good science, good economics and, doubtless, good bar business to withhold judgement on the cause until there is rigorous scientific proof. But being so picky about pinning down cause and effect before offering clear advice is also wildly irresponsible, leaving most of us blind to the mental health impact of alcohol.

Without proper information how can consumers adhere to the drink industry's advice to "drink responsibly"? To omit a clear health warning while championing "corporate responsibility", which foists responsibility on an uninformed consumer, is itself breathtakingly irresponsible. The lack of clear messages is particularly dangerous when people are often brought up to give the benefit of the doubt anyway. Without a clearer message, we will continue to drink alcohol to relax and cheer ourselves up, when all scientific evidence suggests it has exactly the opposite effect.

Since alcohol intake, depression and anxiety, are hard to define, pinpoint in time and quantify, the relationship is always going to be difficult to untangle. It might even be impossible. The diagnosis of alcohol abuse and alcohol dependence are also messy, taking many different forms and having blurred boundaries. Mental health problems like depression and anxiety are at least as slippery. It is not like lung cancer. At what point is feeling low or tense a normal response to difficult circumstances and when is it a medical problem? When did this excessive reaction begin and end? Is it time we all kept a diary? And how does one measure the severity of the symptoms?

To complicate things further, in many societies, if not all, people are often ashamed and fearful of revealing both alcohol problems and mental health problems.

High alcohol consumption, depression and anxiety do not have clear beginnings or ends. They go on over a period of time at varying levels. At times, you might see them to be "normal" reactions to a situation and other times they might seem to be unhealthy. Someone's alcohol intake and state of mind interact with one another. Someone who is feeling sad is "naturally" going to drink more and vice versa. It may not be cause in effect in the sense that one billiard ball causes another billiard ball to change course. But, for the sake of argument, however, alcohol abuse is more likely to come before the onset of five of nine mood and anxiety disorders (MADs), namely: panic, panic with agoraphobia, general anxiety, major depression, and chronic depression.[172] This means alcohol is at least a possible cause of them. Heavy drinking, depression and anxiety frequently coexist, feeding off one another. It could be that neither of them caused of the other, but that they grew up together, perhaps providing conditions in which the other might flourish.

It does not matter which came first MADs or alcohol abuse. Anyone with anxiety or depression who drinks heavily should simply try not drinking for a while to see what happens. The chances are good of enjoying some improvement.

Abstaining does not fix everything, however. Abstainers have been found to be both more and less likely to have problems with depression, depending on which survey you look at. But statistics on abstainers can be misleading, because they are likely to be former alcohol dependents or suffer from an illness, both possible causes of angst. The social exclusion of non-drinkers, particularly those who identify themselves as abstainers, may also play a part in abstainers' gloom.[173] Whatever it is bothering them, the gloomy abstainer would be extremely ill-advised to start drinking alcohol to overcome their woes. ∎

# A diffuse affliction

Even the most committed alcohol advocate is likely to admit there are possible downsides. The negatives can be dramatic, but for the most part their mundanity means they escape our notice, and that of statistics.

We also have a hard time accepting risk as it is measured, preferring our own version of what is risky and what is not. What is the riskiest item in the home for example? Few would say it is the floor, although it is. Nobody wants to go through their lives worrying about floors. Drinking alcohol, like traversing floors, is riskier than we like to think.

It is particularly hard for us to appreciate risk when a negative outcome is hard to define or when the risk changes over time. With alcohol, we tend not to be looking out for negative outcomes because of the positive associations we have for it. And we are unused to an activity where the chances of it doing us harm go up the more we do it. Normally we improve at things we do, and the risk of them backfiring on us goes down. With alcohol it tends to be the opposite.

There are two certainties at the extremes of the statistical scale. If we do not drink, we will not develop alcohol problems. And if we drink enough for long enough, all of us will become alcohol dependent, a state where our brain stops going back to normal after a session. Few of us start out with this as a goal. Instead, we often flirt with heavy drinking, which gives us a big bang for our buck and has fairly subtle immediate impacts. But, session-by-session, we increase the likelihood we will develop dependency. Like driving too fast or on our mobile phones, we might feel perfectly in control, while absentmindedly taking on elevated risk of an accident—physical, psychological or social—and eroding our brain's alcohol recovery capacity. Over time, heavy drinking will tend to steadily reduce our emotional resilience, concentration, impulse control, cognitive flexibility, and planning ability.

Reducing these capacities means that common personal traumas, like the end of a relationship, bereavement, or job loss are a bigger deal for heavy drinkers. We may not have the emotional or cognitive capacity to cope. This kind of situation, in turn, can increase the emotional cues which lead us to drink more, possibly turning a heavy drinker into a dependent one or deepening dependence. After one year of heavy drinking, the chances of developing alcohol dependency are 14 per cent, increasing to 50 per cent after five.[174] The transition from heavy drinking to dependency tends to make life notably grimmer, as we find a trusty stressbuster turning into a new source of stress.

Nobody knows how many unwitting dependents there are because surveys cannot ask us what we do not know. Nevertheless, it seems likely that many of us develop dependency without realising it. The arrival of dependency is not heralded by any great fanfare. It sneaks up steadily over weeks, months, and years. Meanwhile, alcohol's medley of withdrawal symptoms is easily missed or confused with unpleasant feelings which could be attributed to other causes. We might be anxious because of real events or "personality traits" about which we can do nothing. Perhaps we are naturally impulsive, gloomy, sensitive or nervous? Perhaps we have just started to have bad hangovers, rather than developing withdrawal symptoms? This is not the "denial" often talked about in stories about alcohol dependency, it is not knowing.

We tend to prefer explanations which involve the least effort. This approach serves us well in good times, saving us from needless worry and effort. But it can also mean we sometimes avoid explanations which might prove more useful in the long term.

Alcohol dependency is not an easy state to identify, not like a broken arm or a case of chickenpox. It is hard to spot and is different from one person to the next. Some people are plagued by cartoonish cravings to drink, while others are not. We may feel restless and want to get out of the house and meet friends in the pub. This does not, on the face of it, seem like something to be concerned about, but we can sometimes misunderstand our own motives.

There is hardly anyone who has had a drink who has not at some point drunk enough to get inebriated and experienced the uncomfortable comeuppance of a hangover. But how often do you need to do this to qualify as an "alcohol abuser", or heavy drinker, a rung on the boozing ladder which can prefigure dependency? Dependents drink regularly enough to mean their brains do not go back to normal after drinking. We do not have scanners, so the change can only be guessed at from symptoms we might show.

These symptoms form a "cluster" which are present in some dependent drinkers and not in others. Dependent drinkers are, in fact, an extremely diverse bunch. The Diagnostic and Statistical Manual of Mental Disorders (DSM IV), the US diagnosis "bible", defines someone as alcohol dependent if they exhibit three of the following seven symptoms: alcohol tolerance; withdrawal; drink in greater amounts or over a longer time course than intended; desire or unsuccessful attempts to cut down or control use; spent a lot of time drinking or recovering from alcohol use; social, occupational or recreational activities given up or reduced; continued use despite knowledge of physical or psychological consequences of that use.

Crunch the numbers, and there are 99 different ways to be dependent under this definition.[175] There are 35 different ways to be diagnosed with three symptoms; 35 ways to be diagnosed with four; 21 ways to have five, 7 ways to have six and, of course, just one way to have all seven. To confuse matters further the symptoms which contribute to a diagnosis—like "tolerance" or "disruption of normal activities"—are difficult to pin down. So, even if we know the definition, we can be unsure if we qualify. It is not a club where we can expect to have much in common with other members. If we have, say, three symptoms there are five ways you would have no symptom in common with another alcohol-dependent person.[176] And, even when you have symptoms in common, they are still probably not quite the same.

The International Statistical Classification of Diseases (ICD) has a general definition for drug dependence, with alcohol being a special case. It is similar to the US definition but does not say how many of the symptoms we need to have. Instead, it talks of a "cluster of behavioural, cognitive, and physiological phenomena that develop after repeated substance use". It then provides a list of what these might "typically include": a strong desire to take the drug; difficulties controlling the drug's use; persisting in taking the drug despite harmful consequences; a higher priority given to drug use than to other activities and obligations; increased tolerance, and sometimes a physical withdrawal state.[177]

Given the difficulties of diagnosis, it is likely that the vast majority of alcohol dependents go undiagnosed. As many as three-quarters of alcohol dependents who visit a doctor's surgery on other matters are not picked up.[178] Even when an alcohol-dependent person is sitting right in front of them complaining of ill-health, doctors fail to notice. When they do consider the diagnosis, they tend to rely on intuition rather than asking concrete questions, perhaps not wishing to imperil their relationship with a patient. We are remarkably sensitive about it.

Socially there is shame attached to the diagnosis which is taken as an insult. Most people realise the term "dependent" is a euphemism for alcoholic, which people link with foolishness and, perhaps, immorality. The term "dependent" is also misleading in the context of alcohol, seldom meaning we will perish without alcohol, as we would from denying our dependence on food, water or oxygen. Only in very extreme cases are people in any mortal danger from initial withdrawal symptoms. And, as the diagnosis itself says, a dependent drinker is not "at the mercy" of alcohol either, with craving for alcohol not always a symptom.

The answer to just one question can, however, offer a strong clue: Are you a non-daily smoker? A US study found that non-daily smokers are five times as likely to have alcohol problems as people who never smoked.[179] Or, more directly, we might wonder about our "two-day hangover" when we still feel wretched on Monday morning after a boozy Saturday. We might sweat, or feel nauseous, or we might not. We might crave an alcoholic drink, or we might not. Still feeling out-of-sorts after the 24-hours of a hangover is an indication of the withdrawal of dependence.

Dependency would perhaps be better thought of, or even called, "alcohol affliction". We might be afflicted with symptoms of alcohol dependency but have very little to share with others having the same problem. A diagnosis of alcohol dependency is a judgement. But it is a subjective medical judgement, not a moral one. What harm would there be in heavy drinkers pre-empting judgement and assuming anxiety, gloom and cognitive problems like forgetfulness are likely indicators of alcohol dependency or a precursor to it? We can look at the evidence and slow down before crashing the car rather than after.

The final confusion to top it off is that it takes far longer than most of us probably imagine to recover from dependency. When people start drinking, they will just get a hangover lasting less than 24-hours. But the longer people drink, the longer it can take. Practice makes imperfect. Dependent drinkers find a week or two off will provide some significant payoff, but it can take a year and more to be completely rid of dependency symptoms. Even then, a former dependent's brain can still harbour some emotional and cognitive quirks.

For all the complication of the problem, the good news is that the antidote to it, namely not drinking, is simple and inexpensive to prescribe, only it is often found to be quite difficult to take. ■

# Blurred labyrinth

Alcohol problems and dependency are common but identifying them and taking action is not. This is partly because phrases related to alcohol consumption are messy and misunderstood and their application subjective. So, a concrete problem quickly becomes a semantic argument. Many people take the opportunity the confusion offers to ignore the issue and hope for the best, with ill-effects occasionally forcing them to revisit the question.

At what point do we discount our own personal quirks and start to blame problems on booze? Someone who is drunk or hungover is likely to miss something or to make some mistakes. But sober people make mistakes too. You can look for disruption in your life, for instance being late for work or missing family commitments. When does it stop being your misdeeds and when does it start being alcohol? Where is the limit? When does it cross the line to be a problem rather than an amusing accident or trivial nuisance? When does alcohol start "dominating"? And when does our heavy drinking go from being a personal choice to the symptom of dependency? How can you tell what impact alcohol has? How can you tell what impact any one thing has?

In many accounts of alcoholic excess, in books and blogs, the narrator will often say they spend years "denying" they were alcoholics. This is a brave admission to make. But to deny something the truth about it has to be clear to you and, in the case of alcohol dependence, it is often anything but. Alcohol causes problems which vary widely from one person to another, with scores of different combinations, most of which can be attributed to other causes. You cannot meaningfully deny something so unclear. You can, however, come to the wrong judgement, being too inclined to give alcohol the benefit of the doubt.

The boundaries between alcohol problems are vague and debatable, making for a labyrinth of meaning with boundaries that blur. Even experts have differing ideas of what alcohol problems are. In some cases, the problem might be clear, but in cases on the borderline—where most are—there is no way to blame alcohol for our woes without an element of uncertainty. When it is unclear then our habit is generally to give alcohol the benefit of the doubt. So many of us end up damaging ourselves by offering alcohol too much leniency, rather than being denial. Alcohol-leniency is not a cut and dried matter like denial would be, but a combination of misunderstanding and miscalculation.

We have a sample of one person, ourselves, running a one-off psycho-sociological experiment called our life. Few solid conclusions can be drawn from it. So, instead, we have to make do with judgement or guesswork. There is no harm in informing this guesswork, however. And there is plenty of scientific evidence to show regular heavy alcohol drinking tends to diminish our mood and ability to think.

The symptoms of alcohol dependence, when our brains do not reset themselves properly, rather than the social consequences of drinking, are also not easy to pin down. They vary from one person to another. The symptoms also include a rise in our tolerance to alcohol, but we seldom keep track of our drinking closely enough to compare. And we can get better at functioning while inebriated with some mental tricks, without having developed a physical tolerance. Another common symptom of withdrawal of dependence is craving a drink. But what exactly does craving feel like? In reality, your tongue does not hang out at the thought of a cold beer or cocktail, like in a cartoon. How exactly does craving differ from simply feeling like having a drink? Every drinker feels that to some extent, otherwise, they would not have a drink. So, we might ask ourselves, what is wrong with wanting a drink? If we want a drink and have the means to buy it, why not?

Craving might also masquerade as something else. Instead of craving a drink, we might crave going to the pub. Is this not simply a healthy urge to have company and converse after a day's labour? One test we might try might be to see if we can motivate ourselves to go to the pub and not drink alcohol. Even then, however, you might decide the off-putting factor is the teasing you might get from drinking companions for not joining them in drinking alcohol. Alcohol-free beer, which looks like alcoholic beer could be helpful in evading detection, although ordering privately in a public bar presents a challenge.

The complications are reflected in medical definitions too. As we have seen, according to the old American one, the more restrictive of the two, we need to show three or more symptoms from seven. This means there are 99 different hues of alcoholism. And, as we have seen, not even these seven symptoms—which include tolerance and craving—are easily identified. There is good sense in refusing to accept an ill-defined term applies to us, especially when it comes with social stigma and long-term challenges to escape.

To decide we have to change also means casting a critical eye over ourselves. Nobody likes to do that. If we did not exercise scepticism in the face of possible diagnoses, we would risk being overwhelmed with needless worry and hypochondria. We have to accept, however, that we might sometimes live to regret our bravado.

Those who do decide to cut back probably underestimate the amount of time it takes to be rid of alcohol-induced problems. The initial withdrawal is over fairly quickly, but it might take three months to more than a year for cognitive and emotional issues to resolve. Some continue to notice improvements long after. Many people who have cut their drinking will believe they are ready to resume well before that, having felt the immediate relief after the withdrawal phase. Some of the unrecognised alcohol-related niggles, like mood problems, may be among the factors which inspire us to go back to drinking again before they have been allowed the time to disappear.

Alcohol is a parallel universe where we live as we did in the Middle Ages believing word of mouth is more trustworthy than something taken from a scientific journal. What can those ignorant egg-heads know of drinking? We rely mostly on hearsay and wishful thinking.

Declaring ourselves fit to drink is likely to receive hearty approval from our drinking buddies, making it an ever-more tempting option. We do not need to be on the fringes of civilised society to be part of such a group. Village pubs, rugby clubs, golf clubs, and corner bars often provide us with such drinking bands. In many places and professions, it is harder to find a careful drinker than a heavy one. According to one study between 55 and 82 per cent of the total amount of alcohol consumed in the UK was done in a "risky" fashion.[180] And between 22 and 47 per cent of the UK population drink above the government guidelines. So, there are plenty of easy escape routes and support networks if we are thinking of ending our time off alcohol. There are not so many attractive options if we want to stay away from it, although the internet is providing a way to connect.

Sharing a story about drunken hijinks is most likely to be met with comforting, empathetic laughter in the UK. We will, most likely, be rewarded for our openness with a tale of even greater drunken mishap, which makes ours seem reassuringly tame. In the topsy-turvy world of alcohol, the fact that two drinking sessions ended in near-disaster is not confirmation that a problem exists, as it would be in a rational study of the subject, but a problem solved. Both parties feel they are not alone, while each gets what they want. One feels they are not the worst while the other gets to feel top-dog at partying hard.

Sticking to official alcohol guidelines, meanwhile, is widely considered laughable, like keeping to the 70mph speed limit on a UK motorway. Such things are only to be considered by squares and ninnies. It is considered effete, alarmist, or paranoid to be concerned about drinking too much until we are alone, in our underwear, cradling a half-finished bottle of budget vodka between your knees. Then, finally, it may be time to admit there is a problem. The power of stoicism and community spirit is, in many ways, impressive, but it is also the perfect way to ensure "common sense" fail us catastrophically.

Another problem is that the patterns of excessive drinking vary a lot. The stereotype of an alcoholic is a steady dawn-till-dusk swigger, wedded to their hip flask or, perhaps, a man on a park bench surrounded by an army of super-strength lager cans. But this kind of concerted boozing is a rarity among alcohol dependents.

More common among those on the cusp of dependency are committed part-timers who do not drink round the clock but go on a bender once or twice a week, once a month, or blitz the off-licence to cope with a crisis. We do not need to dose our self with alcohol like clockwork to change our brain chemistry. Drinking large amounts of alcohol regularly, in whatever pattern we chose, has the potential to make long-lasting changes to our brains. Binging is one of the more efficient ways to achieve them.

Binging also seems to be an efficient way to make trouble for ourselves and others. A survey of 12,668 German drinkers found problems like repeated family quarrels, loss of partners or friends, and physical fights were more closely linked to a pattern of binge-drinking than to the total volume of alcohol consumed.[181]

Frequent high doses of alcohol have a particularly pronounced impact on the growing brain. This is cruelly ironic because binge drinking is widely seen as a rite of passage in adolescence, a phase of rapid brain development. In one experiment, adolescent primates were used to quantify the effects.[182] An 11-month period of heavy binging in the group led to a significant and persistent reduction in the birth and maturation of new neurons in the hippocampus, the region involved in learning and memory formation. It had a particularly strong effect on the division and migration of hippocampal precursor cells.[183]

The similarities in brain alterations between adolescent binge drinkers and adult alcohol dependents have led some authors to suggest a "continuum hypothesis", in which binge drinking and chronic alcohol dependence are two stages of the same phenomenon.[184] If this is true it is not a binary affair, as people might like to think, with alcoholics on one side, a miserable bunch consigned to a miserable fate, and non-alcoholics on the other, a happily enjoying the benefits of alcohol without serious consequences. It is a jumble of drinking patterns, some apparently controlled, some less so, all causing a degree of acute and chronic brain dysfunction. Being aware that there are a host of subtle and complicated effects connected with alcohol use is more important than which style of drinking we adopt.

The British alcohol industry's information effort, Drink Aware, is well chosen. We should be aware we drink too much if we exceed the government guidelines. We also might usefully be aware we might not feel "addicted" even when we are dependent. We are aware that alcohol can make us feel gloomy or tense, but wrongly imagine that the connection is easily recognised. Feelings and desires do not come with labels of origin attached to make it easy for us. The risk of developing depression, for instance, is not limited to periods before, during, or after having a drink. Binging alone is likely to be a contributory factor to developing depression.[185]

Binging, defined as drinking twice the recommended dose of alcohol at one sitting, is common in many places and not just among adolescents. In the UK, for instance, men binge on around 40 per cent of the times they drink, meaning they drink the equivalent four pints or more large lagers.[186] British women are more restrained, but still binge on a fifth of occasions they drink. Among 16-24-year olds, around a third of men binge on a weekly basis.

The repeated detoxifications that result are linked to cognitive deficits. Female binge drinkers were particularly impaired in vigilance tasks, being less able to inhibit a response to an alerting stimulus. In some tasks, this can be an advantage, like when doing a search and matching task, where binge drinkers showed faster movement time rather than thinking time, indicative of impulsivity in motor response. More tests would be needed to decide to what extent binge drinking might be the cause of such impulsive reactions rather than the effect. Cognitive dysfunctions are unlikely to be entirely due to pre-existing impairments, however, because binging rats have cognitive dysfunctions not seen in their clean-living counterparts.

There could be knock-on effects to binge drinking in terms of drinking habits too. Alcohol-induced impairment of frontal cortex function from repeated detoxifications may make uncontrolled consumption more likely and make it more difficult for abstaining alcohol dependents to resist restarting. It may also, researchers say, have an impact on long-term emotional behaviour. The ability to forgo alcohol for a few days is by no means the all-clear for dependence or enough time for the deficits to disappear.

Repeated detoxification is thought to cause "kindling", in an analogy with the bone-dry material used to start a fire. Alcohol kindling prepares the brain for blazes of convulsant activity, particularly of the amygdala. The amygdala helps us make associations between events in the outside world and the source of our fear reactions.[187] Repeated withdrawals have been shown to increase the hangover symptoms and alcohol-seeking behaviour in animals.[188]

The freedom to have a pattern of binge drinking is considered a birth right in the UK. But it is far less of hearty self-indulgence than noble tradition suggests. Rather than being the way to have the best of both worlds, it seems to ensure that a relatively small amount of alcohol has the most destructive impact possible. ∎

# Processor jamming

"Executive function" might conjure up images of an awkward corporate buffet. But in psychology, it refers to the mental processes in charge of decision-making and planning in changing circumstances.

Executive functions, like the high-ups in a company, are meant to look at the Big Picture, bringing together information and allocating brainpower where it is needed most. It is the top-level management of thought, keeping track of actions, results and prioritising accordingly. It is at this board level that chronic alcohol use seems to have its most damaging effect.

In everyday life, executive functions are engaged when circumstances change, allowing us to adapt to new things.[189] Some activities naturally use them much more heavily than others, like when we make plans or switch from one activity to another, try to resist some instant fun for the sake of a longer-term payoff. Together our executive functions allow us to lead independent, purposeful lives and to be flexible enough to meet the demands of changes when they happen. Without them we would be slaves to our environment, behaving in a fixed way when certain things happen without regard for our goals.

Executive functions seem, on the surface, the antithesis to impulsivity, a trait which alcohol tends to heighten.[190] This might suggest that executive functions serve to make someone's behaviour more conservative or boring. On the contrary, however, they enable us to adapt to new situations. Relying on impulsive responses, by contrast, makes adaptation impossible. So, counterintuitively, an impulsive person with impaired executive functions is unlikely to act in a free-wheeling way when change occurs. They are more likely to be a stick-in-the-mud, unable to adapt. It is, again, not a black-and-white issue, however. No person is completely impulsive nor is anyone without some degree of impulsivity. And an impulsive person can usually suppress some impulses which defeat their goals.

A lot of research has focussed on the types of rigid thinking which can cause harmful levels of alcohol use. It makes sense, of course, to do so because it goes to the heart of the problem of excessive drinking. But changes to executive function also occur in people who only meet the criteria for "hazardous drinking", a type of drinking falling short of dependence. This too can make it more difficult to remember things, make decisions, keep a lid on extraneous thoughts, and ignore distractions.[191] These aggravations may make us drink more, but not necessarily. Drinking to a level where executive functions are diminished can be driven by a lifestyle or routine, rather than being self-perpetuating. Here, where there is relatively little change, the effects may easily go unnoticed.

There is no agreed safe alcohol dose at which full mental functioning is guaranteed.[192] But mental powers are significantly eroded at far lower levels of alcohol consumption than many might like to think. People who drink heavily are prone to around 25 per cent more memory lapses, like forgetting birthdays or paying bills.[193] They also have more deficits in everyday memory, absent-mindedly forgetting things. This can be things like whether we have locked the door or switched off the lights or turn off the oven or mislaying our house keys.

Other studies found that heavy drinkers on the borderline of the UK's alcohol guidelines performed worse on word fluency, some aspects of random letter generation—a test of inhibitory control—and had trouble switching between tasks.[194] If we drink enough to qualify for an alcohol use disorder, meanwhile, we are likely to have greater trouble guessing what other people are thinking.[195] This lack of empathy can, of course, make social relations more difficult to maintain.

It does not take very long for heavier drinking to have an effect on executive functions either. Teenage students who had a habit of binge drinking showed a larger spike of electrical activity when an "oddball" image was inserted into a stream of images, which suggests they had a problem with their working memory.[196] It seems their brains were having to co-opt bits of their brain not needed by non-bingers. The differences between the brain response of binge drinkers and their more abstemious peers grew larger over two years.

Teenage drinkers who had graduated from binge drinking to the ranks of alcohol dependents were found to have already physically shrunk parts their brains.[197] The effect was most noticeable in the volume of the hippocampus and prefrontal cortex, the effect being more pronounced in female subjects.[198] Previously, these abnormalities had been found only in "seasoned" middle-aged drinkers. Curiously, the more a young woman drinks, the less able they are to detect facial symmetry when sober.[199]

There is uncertainty over cause and effect because drinkers may drink because they have mental deficiencies. But, on balance, it seems that the damage we suffer is likely to be related to the volume we drink. As a rough guide: Drinking five or six US "standard drinks"—that's three-and-a-half to four large beers—a day for extended periods is likely to cause "cognitive inefficiencies"; Five or six beers a day, meanwhile, is a recipe for "mild cognitive deficits"; And drinking seven or more drinks a day is likely to impair our cognition to a level normally seen in people diagnosed as having alcohol dependence. In other studies people drinking an averaging of 418g of alcohol week, or an average of about three large beers a day, tended to show reduced frontal lobe volume, whereas those who consumed 181g or less did not.[200] The effects of binging are harder to quantify.

While light-to-moderate alcohol drinking seems to reduce the likelihood of dementia, attempting to stick to the measly ration needed to see such protective effects is perilous for those who have learned to enjoy inebriation.[201] Drinking beyond a very moderate level seems to diminish whatever brainpower we have.

The executive functions are mainly performed in the prefrontal cortex, the outer layer at the front of our brain, but parts of the brain's interior are also thought to play a role.

As is often the case, the physical location of different brain functions has been deduced by observing the problems of people who have bits of their brain missing. Those of us with the back two-thirds of our pre-frontal cortex destroyed by trauma or disease have trouble with executive functions like concentrating, orienting themselves, abstract thought, judgment and problem solving, resolving conflicting thoughts, and planning. Those of us who lose the front part of our pre-frontal cortex, meanwhile, lose the executive functions which help overcome our urges. This means we can engage in unruly social behaviour.[202] The prefrontal cortex is the part of the brain which is most affected by alcohol.[203] So, it is not altogether surprising that executive functions located here are the ones shown to be impaired by alcohol use when seen using computed tomography and magnetic resonance images.

Studies have reported a decreased level of frontal lobe glucose utilisation and reduced cerebral blood flow in dependent drinkers. Another study found reduced levels of dopamine neurotransmitter in the synapses of newly-abstinent alcoholics, another possible reason for their relatively poor executive function performance.[204]  People who get an unusually high boost of dopamine when they drink—like those with the 118G receptor variant—might have a dopamine rebound when they sober up. Researchers have also observed lower levels of dopamine in the striatum, a part of the forebrain which may also play a part in executive functions. Other neuropsychological studies found that there are specific deficits in alcohol dependents which suggest frontal lobe dysfunction.

The frontal lobe is, however, not an isolated region of the brain, being massively connected to other cortical and subcortical areas. Glutamate, the neurotransmitter alcohol suppresses, also plays a pivotal role in executive functions. Binge drinkers, unlike slow-and-steady drinkers, see a large rise in glutamate when they drink, sometimes rising to four or five times the normal level[205]. This glutamate glut during a binge may backfire when we sober up, with neurons adjusting to the oversupply by reducing our sensitivity to the transmitter. This insensitivity to glutamate could reduce our ability to learn. This is not good news for students.

Once again it is rodents which hint at this possibility. Blocking glutamate's role in transmission in the prefrontal cortex and striatum of mice meant they performed less well in learning tasks where they would be rewarded with food if they touched a screen showing a particular certain image. Turning off the glutamate system in their dorsal striatal markedly slowed their ability to learn, while shutting it off in the prefrontal cortex made the mice less able to adapt to a new reward image. Mice, whose lives are typically far less complicated than ours, are also far less dependent on their prefrontal cortex. We probably make more decisions in a minute than a mouse does in a lifetime, and more complicated ones too, requiring more computation than simply acting on a cue.

The possibility that alcohol promotes rigid thinking and an inability to learn is potentially significant if we want to change our habits. We can find it particularly hard to shift from consuming alcohol to other sources of reward. But it also suggests a mechanism which stops heavy drinkers, who are below the criteria for dependence, from changing their behaviour. As heavy drinkers, we may go on repeating behaviour which is unrewarded for longer than we might otherwise. Drinking alcohol can be its own reward. And alcohol can undermine our capacity to take hints from other people, examine evidence, and make decisions.

The decrease in medial frontal cortex glucose metabolism found in alcohol-dependent people has been correlated with poor performance in the Wisconsin Card Sorting Task. In this game, we are asked to sort cards into different piles according to a rule which can change from one minute to the next without warning. Time is of the essence. The sorting rule can be based on the shape of the pictures on the cards, their colour, or the number of symbols. The person doing the test has to deduce the rule change from being told if they have put their card on the right pile. Imaging research has shown that the test not only measures the performance of the prefrontal cortex but other regions of the brain too.[206] In real life, it might mean we might pull a door-handle with "push" written on it.

The good news is that frontal glucose metabolism increases after a period of abstinence which may mean that some of the consequences of long-term alcohol use are reversible. It is not clear if other changes to the prefrontal cortex are reversible, however. In one study, subjects abstinent for between six and nine months showed no increase in frontal lobe volume compared to when they began their abstinence. Other studies are not so encouraging either.[207] One test took a sample of 47 people, roughly half of them classified as dependent, half of them abstinent. Poorer cognitive performance was directly related to the level of alcohol craving they felt and their years of alcohol dependence. It did not improve with the number of years of abstinence. Another study showed some alcohol-dependent subjects had deficits in a gambling task similar to patients with lesions of the prefrontal cortex.[208]

Other experiments have found long-term alcohol overuse to be more detrimental to attention and executive functioning than cocaine. And heavy drinking alone has been found to be enough to have an impact on fractionated executive processes: updating, shifting, inhibition and access to semantic memory.[209] Even when dependent drinkers do not show deficits in certain executive functions, the prefrontal cortex seems to go about tasks in a different way. Binge drinking adolescents too have workarounds. They performed adequately in visual working memory tasks, but with reduced activation in the right anterior prefrontal cortex. The difference may show up when more complex cognitive functions are required.

The frequency, complexity, and impact of the decisions required of us are, arguably, increasing. Our jobs and personal relationships are more fluid than ever before. The spread of technology, meanwhile, requires us to absorb and dispense ever-more information, magnifying the impact of our errors just as efficiently as our successes. Using email or social media we have the capacity to irritate or impress in equal measure. An ill-considered post to Facebook or Twitter is, these days, enough to cause an uproar, even a court case, the same joke in the local pub would not.

All of these place an extra burden on our abilities to learn, make decisions and adapt to change. This is what our executive functions are for. Arguably, then, it is a particularly bad time to be drinking alcohol. It offers us a blessed relief from the demands on our executive functions but can quickly become the mental equivalent of going out to play football in lead boots. ∎

# Where there's a will

Inebriation and dependency put into question the extent to which we can control our actions. This is a special case of the question of "free will", one of philosophy's most baffling conundrums.

It seems there is never going to be a definitive answer to whether we are making choices, or we might be just imagining it. Unanswerable as it may be, this does not stop us from speculating. And the results of our speculation are important, no matter whether we are philosophers or normal people. What we believe about free will is a factor in our ability to control our behaviour, including our alcohol intake. Believing we have no will, accepting we are simply part of a cosmic pinball machine makes it harder to control our behaviour. Feeling we have the ability to forge our own path makes it easier. This does not prove the existence or otherwise of free will, but demonstrates the importance of our beliefs about it.

Perhaps because of this curious effect, the definition of addiction been in orbit around free will since it was coined. The term "addiction"— from the Latin *ad dicare*, to submit to something—was first used by Shakespeare. For three centuries or so, it meant only a strong liking for something but then, around 1900, it started to become a medical term applied specifically to a strong inclination to take a drug. A view took hold among some people that addicted people could not resist taking the drug to which they were addicted, meaning they had effectively lost their free will. Put in these extreme terms, however, addiction is a Catch-22 situation for the addict, where the solution to the problem is denied by the problem. Being "addicted", according to this definition, means lacking the will needed to be free of it. Welcome, then, to a pit of despair.

Even the current term of alcohol "dependence" leans in this direction too, though it is meant to be less pejorative than alcoholic. But "dependence" on alcohol is not the same thing as dependence on water or food, because we will not perish without it. In the worst case, we may have withdrawal symptoms which require hospital treatment.

 Seeing alcohol dependence as a disease over which we have no control has avoided unhelpful moralising where alcohol dependents have been told they are weak or evil. But telling someone they are helpless is also against their interest. Undermining our confidence in our ability to exercise control over our behaviour, which makes it more difficult to be rid of behavioural problems like dependence. It is perfectly reasonable, then, to resist this disempowered view of ourselves, but that can make it more difficult for others to help.

Our default setting is that of feeling we have control over their lives, with 60 per cent or more saying they have it.[210] We like the feeling of being in control of things. Sports, games, playing music, painting, dancing, drama, art, and work all provide situations in which we can enjoy the feeling of making choices, taking action, and seeing the effect. We even enjoy watching other people exert their free will, whether in a sport, drama, or everyday people watching. It seems we are hardwired to enjoy these things. It seems silly to deny ourselves a pleasure which appears helpful to our well-being.

Alcohol inebriation offers us an arena in which we can express our free will too, simplifying the menu of options we have to what we have in front of us. Our decision-making abilities are diminished and our criteria for satisfaction more modest. This gives a heightened appreciation of being in command.

But, for all our limitations while inebriated, we do not suddenly lose free will because of alcohol. In fact, life of heavy drinking requires far more willpower than a sober one. Imagine the extra effort required to get up and struggle into work on a hangover or make it to football practice on a Sunday morning. No-one could manage such feats who did not have both a strong will and the ability to impose it. It is wrong then to question the capacity for wilful behaviour of someone who drinks a lot, even if the drinking and its consequences are unintended.

For the most part, we feel we "need a drink" because it seems preferable to being sober. The potential discomforts of being might include everyday worries or boredom, discomforts which alcohol can relieve, only making them worse later. Even if the discomfort is extreme, as it can be, alcohol dependence is the expression of a preference for inebriation rather than being an unavoidable outcome. A dependent drinker's brain has adapted to make the inebriated state more pleasant than the sober one, perhaps much more. A heavy drinker between sessions can experience alcohol-induced unease or "anhedonia", the inability to feel pleasure, or feelings of woe. They may also hanker for a drink to end these irksome feelings.

Once inebriated alcohol myopia gives greater significance to immediate rewards, which are likely to include alcohol. The here and now of drinking in a bar will often include cues to take the payoff of having another drink. These cues will take the form of marketing material and entertainment that might end if our glass falls empty. We might well give into these cues. But being inclined to be inebriated, or more so, still does not from a lack of will, because a choice is still being made. It is just that we are heavily biased towards that decision.

Can decisions, skewed as the result of alcohol exposure and a persuasive environment, actually become pre-determined? Can we always exert our will to override the bias towards having a drink? The answer seems to be: Yes, we can. It is possible, although circumstances can make it excruciatingly difficult.

Alcoholics Anonymous (AA), a group which aims to help alcohol-dependent people, insists its members say they are powerless over alcohol. Step one of its manual *Twelve Steps to Recovery*, which members are meant to sign up, reads: "We admitted that we were powerless over alcohol, that our lives had become unmanageable."[211] Initiates are then required to hand over their fate to a "higher power". It is unclear, however, how someone who is powerless can hand power to anyone or anything, higher or not. We cannot give what we claim we do not have unless we are dealing in complex financial derivatives. Scientists too often argue that free will is a delusion and that all human actions are the consequence of prior events.[212] They cannot know this.

True or not, such fatalistic views are potentially dangerous for people who have trouble controlling their behaviour. A loss of belief in free will, induced in the lab by reading text which argue against its existence, makes it harder for us to control our behaviour. It has also been shown to lead us to increased levels of cheating, stealing, aggression, and to be less helpful.[213] Disbelieving in free will also make people less likely to think for themselves, conforming more readily to other people's judgments, and less willing to draw lessons from our own misbehaviour.[214] The benefits of believing in free will only goes so far, though. People with supreme belief in their autonomy do not become saints or supermen. Boosting our belief in free will does not improve our behaviour beyond that of the norm.

As a rule, we tend to be quite cynical about what we believe, moulding our philosophy to suit our immediate interests. This goes for free will too. If we reflect on our past misdeeds and start to feel guilty, we tend to prefer deterministic views over belief in free will.[215] This means we need not worry about the negative impact of our decisions because they were not ours to make. As the researchers put it: "If asked to choose between 'I freely choose to indulge in unproductive pleasures instead of discharging my social responsibilities' versus 'I am a helpless victim of biological forces and inherently dangerous foreign substances,' many people will understandably prefer the latter."

Crossing the line from a deterministic view and one where free will holds can mean re-evaluating events and accepting our mistakes. Perhaps some of these mistakes were made while impaired by inebriation. We have the capacity to make such a re-evaluation fairly.

Oddly the inebriated seem more decisive and wilful than the sober. The normally timid and anxious can make what appear to be bold decision after a few drinks. An introvert may, with a single bound, feel free to take centre stage, defying their normal insecurities.

Allowing alcohol to subdue our mental gremlins can offer a glorious sense of personal freedom. There is the thrill of acting and making an impact without the need to make choices or messy compromises, as we do in daily life. And alcohol even provides a ready-made excuse for misjudgements. This, however, can also backfire. Alcohol does not allow us to overcome or alter the thoughts which act as self-restraints. It makes us temporarily blind to them. Actions based on the reduced data of inebriation are not the same as decisions made sober. We are bolder when inebriated because our perception and decision-making capacity has been disabled, not because our bravery has increased.

Alcohol is so pervasive that decisions about its consumption are often made without knowing the true reason. Are we sad to be missing a social event or are we sad to miss a drink? Feelings and thoughts do not come with a label of origin. Meeting friends is a real human need, and it is also the perfect excuse to have a drink. The misunderstanding of our own motives is easy to make.

It does not make much practical sense to question the existence of our will but might still help to be clearer on what free will might be and what its limits are.

There are three basic positions. On one wing are the "hard determinists" who say free will is an illusion and that all human behaviour, thoughts, feelings, decisions, and everything else in the world is preordained. The feeling of making a decision is, according to them, a predetermined feeling in a universe in which everything is on rails. Libertarians, on the other wing, say human behaviour, thoughts, and feelings are not predetermined, and the universe is not on a predetermined path. People, they say, can make decisions which alter its course. And, then, there is the centre ground, called "compatibilism", probably the hardest to understand. Compatibilists say the will can operate freely regardless of whether determinism is true. We, they believe, can make choices even though our thoughts and actions have causes. Freedom, in their view, is not an absence of causation but an absence of compulsion.

It is hard to get our heads around. But it matters because, if the hard determinists were right and the universe and its inhabitants are on some predetermined course, then no actions would be free. It would not matter if someone was alcohol dependent or not, they would have no control of their actions. Free will would just be an illusion. The "normal" drinker or gambler would be no more free or constrained than the "addict". They would both just have been dealing with the consequences of different initial conditions. A dependent would have the misfortune to be on a trajectory to have another drink and there would be nothing they could do about it. It would be a matter of fate, with no need to consider it further.

For libertarians and compatibilists, meanwhile, people can choose some outcomes. The complicated part comes in deciding on the degree of control people have, given a set of circumstances. Even for them circumstances can conspire to mean someone is not able to control their destiny. Having a piano fall on our head from an upstairs window is not fair to chalk it up as the result of choosing a bad moment to step out for a stroll. It was a misfortune beyond our control. Most of us will make an orbit of the sun in the next 12 months, whether we want to or not. Some outcomes are decided with our say-so while others are not.

So, the issue is not black-and-white. It is impossible to say which outcomes are the result of our choice and, of those which are, which was the result of alcohol consumption. All you can do is make an educated guess, which is one reason the consequences and causes of alcohol consumption are so difficult to identify.

"Oh, don't let him [or her] bother you, he is drunk," is a widely employed excuse. Sadly, however, forgiveness may avoid social awkwardness but does not repair the cost of someone's misbehaviour. You cannot be un-insulted, or unthumped, or de-runover.

*Top Gear* presenter Jeremy Clarkson, an idol for many boys and men, was given a relatively easy time by the public for thumping a junior colleague in 2015 because it was suggested he was drunk when he did it. If he had been understood to be sober, he would have had a far more difficult time. If he was drunk, well, "These things happen." But the law and the BBC did not provide Clarkson with protection on the grounds of drunkenness, although inebriation may have been a factor. He and his colleagues are now presenting their car show on Amazon. A plea of drunk would, otherwise, be a safe haven for all manner of miscreants.

While we are prepared to forgive, we cannot afford to issue get out of jail free cards. That would be inviting trouble. The law courts take little notice of whether or not we have been drinking when coming to a verdict on our behaviour. Practice varies from one country to the next but seldom do judges consider being inebriated an excuse, even though our reasoning and emotions can be seriously affected.

On the whole, laws say someone made the decision to be drunk and what happens subsequently is their fault. This includes alcohol dependents who find it hard not to drink. In 1988, the US Supreme Court found alcoholism to be the result of the alcoholics' "own wilful misconduct". It reaffirmed a lower court ruling that there exists "a substantial body of medical literature that even contests the proposition that alcoholism is a disease, much less that it is a disease for which the victim bears no responsibility."[216] It is true we all have control over our inebriation, albeit unreliable. But we cannot control the circumstances we find ourselves in afterwards.

A huge number of crimes are committed while inebriated, perhaps a third or more. Around half of murderers are intoxicated at the time they killed, as were their victims.[217] It also plays a part in around half of all violent crimes and sexual assaults worldwide.[218] People who become very drunk once or more a year are involved in violence approximately twice as often as perennially moderate drinkers.[219] Alcohol-dependent men, meanwhile, are violent to women significantly more often than non-dependent men. Some violence in which alcohol is involved is not illegal. Between ten and twenty per cent of alcohol-dependent people kill themselves, a rate of over 5,000 times that of the general population.[220] This does not count all the other non-fatal ways those of us with alcohol problems hurt themselves and others. US college health authorities say alcohol is the biggest date rape drug, with alcohol being the drug present in 77 per cent of rape cases where the victim was chemically incapacitated.[221]

But most heavy drinkers do not find themselves formally judged by a court. This does not mean they evade the stern judgement of friends, relatives, acquaintances or employers. A rap sheet of missed meeting, arguments, betrayals, fights, or ill-judged remarks can all add up to a reputation for unreliability, or worse.

This is not necessarily any better than legal punishment. Heavy drinkers may accumulate many such experiences. Making sense of them all may not be easy, particularly if they also have impaired memories, heightened fear responses, anxiety, low mood, and impulsive tendencies. This does not add up to a happy situation.

As well as being an agent of some seriously bad behaviour, alcohol can also be seen as a truth serum. It is a paradox typical of our overwhelmingly forgiving attitude toward alcohol. Inebriation can blind us from factors which would normally prevent us from saying things, so we say them anyway. Some believe this means it can offer a glimpse behind someone's public mask. "In wine there is truth," as the Greeks put it. Alcohol is then a kind of liquid Wikileaks, prompting us to make stunning revelations. It is debatable whether such a lack of forethought is a good thing. Whether a revelation made with without regard for the consequences turns out for the best is a matter of chance.

If we are more open and truthful when drunk then, logically enough, we must be more uptight and less genuine when sober. It is true a lot of us really do loosen up. But is it really a good idea to get to know someone when they are not behaving as they would normally? Might it not be better to find people who can be open and relaxed when they are sober.

Inebriation does not make us any more or less slaves to the laws of physics. What it does is reduce the range of factors we consider when we make our choices, meaning we can make different decisions than we would sober. Something which seemed like a good idea at the time, then, can naturally seem misguided when we have sobered up. Excluding information from our decision-making can sometimes lead us down interesting and exciting new paths, although they are not guaranteed to lead somewhere we want to go.

Alcohol's effect on our capacity for decision-making can continue after our blood-alcohol levels drop to normal. Getting inebriated regularly over months or years can mean our brains adapt to functioning better when there is elevated alcohol in our bloodstream. This adaptation can mean we have depleted emotional and cognitive resources when our blood-alcohol is normal.

Being emotionally sensitive, as this adaptation can mean, may bias us towards choices which avoid challenges. Cognitive deficiencies, meanwhile, may limit our ability to create and carry out complex plans, as does a tendency to act more impulsively. All these factors are likely to change the outcome of our decisions one way or another. We can stumble upon lucky breaks, while unexpectedly losing out on the rewards we have worked for.

Limping from one hangover to the next, our ability to fulfil, or perhaps even remember, our promises can be impaired too. In practice, this means we can start to undermine the trust people place in us, downgrading our relationships. Often these shortcomings can be written-off. But, ultimately, a lifestyle of regular benders and a social network dominated by other heavy drinkers can mean we become an unreliable cog in an unreliable social machine.

It is generally not a moral issue at stake here, but a blundering issue. Trust operates like an invisible currency, and we risk losing our ability to accumulate it. Being able to offer undertakings that are believed is what allows us to participate in this trade and to be valued in a social group. The disruptions of heavy drinking can make us increasingly unreliable. So, little-by-little, we might find ourselves pushed further to the fringes.

Alcohol makes us feel more in command of the moment, while it can steadily reduce our ability to control our future. There is excitement in making this trade-off, but like most gambles, it cannot be guaranteed to pay off long term. ■

# Wilfully ill?

Doctors have now, mercifully, put down their medicinal cocktail shakers to focus on treating liver damage and alcohol dependence, rather than being one of the causes of it.

Deciding if consuming too much alcohol is a disease like others is a long and tortured debate. The issue hinges on how much control we have over our drinking, which touches again on the issue of free will. If alcohol-dependent people have a choice to drink, then doctors might have no business treating it. It may be very hard for us to resist the urge to have a drink, but no amount of willpower will rid us of a broken leg, bunions, or chickenpox. On the other hand, many of us continue drinking despite saying we want to stop, so how free are we? Can drinking be so hard to resist that it is, for practical purposes, an involuntary illness?

This has practical consequences because it decides the type of medical help alcohol dependents can get and whether health insurers or health services will underwrite the cost. If our alcohol dependence is not under our wilful control we are likely to get more help to stop. As mentioned previously, some popular counselling services, like Alcoholics Anonymous, require people to say they lack control over their drinking right at the start.

There is a middle road, however. Dependency is neither a disease beyond someone's control or an act of wilful self-harm. It is something in-between. It is something like Type II diabetes, where a genetic vulnerability is exacerbated by our dietary choices. As with Type II diabetics, our position on the continuum of alcohol use depends on the combination of the brain and body we were born with and the choices we make.

Alcohol problems then can be seen as a chemically-induced learning difficulty which restricts and reorders the desirability of the menu of choices we have. We are still able to choose between the options, but it heavily biases our choice in favour of drinking. Alcohol-dependent brains give alcohol drinking a special ticket allowing it to jump to the head of the queue. It does not matter what the other options are, they just don't have alcohol's special pass.

A dependent can make other choices but doing so means dragging alcohol back from the front of the queue, which requires effort. Our environment and sobriety, or otherwise, makes the job more or less difficult. A typical barroom, together with the restricted worldview of intoxication means there are few alternatives to put ahead of drinking. In other, easier situations there are relatively few things suggesting a drink or allowing us to have one. So, a learning difficulty can be more difficult to overcome in some environments than others. Environments bristling with alcohol advertising or other cues to drink are not helpful for us if we have a learning difficulty or for preventing them developing in others.

Recognising a difficulty making choices about drinking is far more helpful for alcohol-dependent people than saying they are completely helpless. A learning difficulty might bias us towards a particular choice, but it remains a choice. It also means that alcohol dependent or not, many of us can sympathise with the situation. Non-dependent drinkers too often get "carried away" and have one too many, giving an insight into the difficulties of dependent people, whose difficulty is simply carried on into normal life.

The learning difficulty may sometimes come because alcohol has the capacity to deliver an isolated element of what is normally a sealed unit of motivation. As mentioned in previous chapters, genetically susceptible people and strains of other species experience a boost in the levels of a brain-signalling substance called dopamine when they drink. Dopamine seems not to be responsible for "liking" or pleasure, as we are often told, but "wanting", a drive to have something which does not necessarily feel good. This is an extremely confusing element to introduce into our recreation time.

Wanting without liking like this is not normally parachuted into our lives. It might normally be something we get from work or doing our household chores like the ironing. Dopamine release is a precursor to action towards a goal, but that goal does not need to be one which promises pleasure. We get a dopamine release to spur us to take action to avoid something nasty too. So, there is no reason why our drinking alcohol should be accompanied by any foreseeable pleasure if our brains are giving us a shot of dopamine when we drink.

We might drink simply because dopamine has circled it in red pen on our to-do list. It may seem worthwhile, somehow. Perhaps this is also part of the reason drinking may often look like happiness from the outside, without necessarily bringing it to those who participate regularly.

Dependent drinkers are at the mercy of similar confusions to those of session drinkers on a roll, only more of the time. Heavy drinking and dependence are, perhaps, best not seen as satisfying some greedy, hedonistic thirst, as widely imagined, but as cycles of perpetually-unfulfilled want. It is up to us to discern the difference. ■

# Splitting the spectrum

Our alcohol drinking is periodic, with an intensity which changes over time. This means we can only be placed somewhere on a spectrum of common alcohol consumption patterns.

Statistical data tends to ignore the dynamic, often chaotic nature of drinking at the individual level, which is typically far from stable or systematic.[222] What we drink one day depends on what we drank the day before, on who we are with and on conscious efforts to cut down or stave-off withdrawal symptoms. Some scientists have even attempted to apply the mathematics of chaos theory to a drinker's intake to understand what is going on. This has just scratched the surface. Chaos is hard to control or define, particularly if you happen to be inebriated, hungover or in withdrawal.

Non-drinkers are oddballs in the West, but not so worldwide. Nearly two-thirds of the world's population has not had a drop in the past year.[223] The average alcohol drinker, meanwhile, gets through 6.2 litres of alcohol a year, or 17ml a day, or 1.7 UK units. If people consistently drank at that level, there would be no need for a book about it, let alone a shelf of them. Adding up to 12 units a week, this average is just below the UK's 14-unit weekly maximum recommendation for both men and women introduced at the start of 20. But people do not drink in this uniform way at all. It varies enormously between nationalities and within social groups.

There are some broad patterns, however. Wealthier people tend to drink more, with Europeans being some of the most enthusiastic alcohol guzzlers. The average EU citizen gets through an average of 30ml a day, bang on the male UK maximum, if we ignore that the abstainers pull the figure down. European alcohol consumption has fallen by nearly 30 per cent since a peak in the 70s but is still higher than after World War Two. Excluding abstainers, European drinkers overshoot the UK maximum level for men by an average of 36 per cent. North Americans are not far behind with around 30 per cent of the US population drinking more than the recommended maximum.[224] Abstaining is a minority sport in both continents. In Europe, around 15 per cent of the population are dry, while 25 per cent are in the US.[225]

Different nationalities within Europe drink quite differently, with fewer southern Europeans than other nationalities reporting getting drunk each month. Northern and eastern Europeans, however, make no bones about getting periodically plastered. In practically all countries, there tends to be a group of die-hard drinkers who drink far more than everyone else. In EU countries, the alcohol drinkers in the top 10 per cent of alcohol consumption get through between a third and half of the total volume of alcohol consumed.[226]

The traditional southern European drinking pattern is characterised by almost daily consumption of wine, often with meals, with little irregular heavy drinking. In central Europe, people drink more beer, drink more outside mealtimes, but still tend to avoid heavy drinking sessions. In northern and Eastern Europe, however, people tend not to drink every day and instead drink heavily outside mealtimes, often very heavily. They are more often session drinkers than steady drinkers.

In the EU15, the precursor to the current 28-member EU, adults said they were drunk five times a year, but binged 17 times by drinking five or more drinks. That means 40 million EU15 citizens have been drunk each month and 100m, a third of the total, binge once a month. The likelihood of developing alcohol dependency or other alcohol problems tends to increase in line with the regularity of someone going over the daily guideline maximums.

There is a significant minority of people elsewhere who drink alcohol with enough gusto to become dependent. Around 140 million people, or around 2 per cent of the world's population, are thought to be dependent, according to the World Health Organisation. Dependency seems to go hand-in-hand with a dip in quality of life greater than that starting to smoke tobacco or using illegal drugs.[227] The proportion of dependents in the United States and Western Europe is much higher than the world average, with between 10 to 20 per cent of men and 5 to 10 per cent of women are thought to have met the criteria for alcohol dependence at some point in their lives.[228]

The US provides the most detailed picture of the shifts within its drinking population. Around half of its alcohol dependents are young adults, with an average age of 22. Just over half of these newly-minted dependents have relatively few problems and will grow out of them.[229] Few of them abuse other drugs, suffer from mental disorders or have family members with alcohol problems. They rarely seek or seemingly need, any kind of help. The remainder of these young alcohol abusers, however, have more difficulty. They have often started drinking early and often come from families with alcohol problems. Around half of them have a psychiatric diagnosis of Antisocial Personality Disorder—being "difficult" in more ordinary parlance—and many have major depression, bipolar disorder, or anxiety problems. Two-thirds of this group of troubled young dependents smoke cigarettes and marijuana, and many also have cocaine and opiate addictions. Around a third look for help in curbing their drinking.

The remaining half of US alcohol dependents, besides young tearaways, are mostly middle-aged or older. Two-fifths of them are well-educated and have stable jobs and families. Many have family histories of alcoholism. About a quarter have had a major depressive illness at some time and almost half were cigarette smokers at some point. A second two-fifths have additional difficulties. Most of this group smoke cigarettes and nearly one-in-five take cocaine or marijuana. A quarter of this second two-fifths sought treatment for their problem drinking, more than twice the average rate among alcohol-dependent people.

And then there are the most hardcore of all, making up the remaining fifth of older US dependents. They too are mostly middle-aged and developed alcohol problems early and have high rates of Antisocial Personality Disorder and criminality. Almost 80 per cent of them come from families with alcohol problems. They have unusually high level of mental disorders, including depression and anxiety, along with a high rate of cigarette smoking. They are also more prone to using marijuana, cocaine, and opiates. Two-thirds of them seek treatment, six times the average among all dependents, enough to make them the largest group among treatment-seekers, despite being a small minority of alcohol dependents.

Help, it seems, does often reach people who need it the most. But most people do not receive treatment, and those who do often only get it well after their problem developed, a span of time known as the "lost decade". Low levels of treatment and diagnosis are also common in mental health problems, which are stigmatised and often thought something we should face unaided. The small percentage of Americans who received help with alcohol drinking only did so eight years after their dependence began. Only 7 per cent of people who abuse alcohol in America ever receive help, with fewer than one in nine alcohol dependents seeing a need for it.[230] Of those who graduated from abuse to alcohol dependence, only one-in-four had some kind of treatment. The percentage of treatment-seekers has remained fairly steady but has fallen slightly since the early 90s. It may be no bad thing for so many people to go it alone. A 1993 study of a sample of 126 problem drinkers found that help-seeking and attaining abstinence are "somewhat independent processes".[231]

There are fewer statistics available in the EU, thanks mostly to its administrative and linguistic divisions. But across Europe, the percentage of alcohol-dependent people receiving treatment was around half that of the US, at around 10 per cent.[232] Taken together, however, there is a European alcohol-dependent population of one-in-twenty men and around one-in-seventy women. This is a total of 12 million people, more people than the population of Belgium. The prevalence of alcohol dependence follows the pattern of drinking habits. In the relatively careful drinking culture of Italy, there are fewer than 1 per cent dependents. But in the hard-drinking Nordic countries, the rate is 7.4 per cent for men and 2.7 per cent for women and 7.8 per cent for men and 1.5 per cent for women in the east. In the centre and west of Europe, it was 6.2 per cent for men and 1.9 per cent for women.

In the UK, 5 per cent of adults "show some signs of alcohol dependence", according to Alcohol Concern. This fairly low estimate works out at about 1.6 million people. Around 250,000 of them are estimated to be moderately to severely dependent to the point they might benefit from specialist treatment. Around 44 per cent of these dependent adult drinkers were in treatment in

England in 2013-14.[233] Forgetfulness, shame, and not recognising the diverse symptoms of dependence may mean self-reported statistics are on the low side. A third of Americans, meanwhile, said alcohol drinking was a nuisance at some point in their lives and around 7 per cent (17 million) consider it a nuisance at any given time.[234]

The percentage of dependent drinkers tends to remain stable, but the people in the group change. We do not have alcohol problems for life nor do we have lifelong immunity.

The nature of the inflows and outflows from dependence can only be guessed at. Like in physics, where over 90 per cent of the matter in the universe has yet to be seen, people who study alcohol cannot see the vast majority of alcohol dependents. They tend to see the small minority of drinkers who come forward to receive treatment, perhaps less than 10 per cent of the total dependents. Useful as it is, studies of those of us receiving treatment may not always shed useful light on the 90 per cent outside it.

Some studies have, however, managed to take stock of the movement of alcohol dependents roaming free.[235] Many seem to find ways to handle their alcohol problem themselves. A 1981 study of 96 alcoholics in Lundby, a suburb of the Swedish city of Gothenburg, found 41 per cent of untreated alcoholics had become either abstainers or had moderated their drinking after 15 years. And a study in Ontario, Canada, found three-quarters of people who had reported problems with drinking had it under control without treatment.[236] Over half of the Ontarians who had got to grips with

their drinking had switched to a lower, non-abusive level of drinking, though many drank at a level with a high incidence of relapse.

The Ontario study also showed women to be more successful at curbing alcohol use than men, while being married seems to help put the dampers on heavy drinking by both sexes. A higher level of education also seems to correlate with successful non-abstinent recovery, but was also negatively associated with abstinent recovery, as does an absence of abstemious friends. Non-abstinent recovery also proved harder for people who were more dependent to begin with. But those who were more dependent had a better chance of achieving abstinent recovery compared to continued dependence, relapse, or non-abstinent recovery. The older you are when you become dependent, the easier it becomes to wean yourself off. The message from both Lundby and Ontario was loud and clear for those wanting a speedy recovery from dependency: it is best to start when you are an old, married woman with a circle of abstemious friends.

The DIY approach is quite successful. A study of Germans attempting to rid themselves of alcohol dependency found over 80 per cent managed to stick with the programme for a year.[237] Giving up alcohol is easier for some people than others for reasons beyond our control. Rats with genetic inclinations to drink were found to go back to drinking after being subjected to relatively modest stress.[238] Another large genetic group, men, seems particularly prone to reaching for the bottle when they get upset.[239]

A large survey of American drinkers came up with similarly encouraging results to those in Sweden and Canada. Around 4,400 had an alcohol dependence which had begun more than a year before the survey. Most of them were middle-aged white men, more than half of them married or living with someone. Around two-thirds had attended or completed college and three quarters had families with a history of alcoholism. This could be the result of a genetic link, but it might also be down to upbringing, or a bit of both. A third of them said they were sinking eight or more drinks a day during their heaviest drinking periods, equivalent to around three or four large beers. Most of them had at some point used tobacco or illegal drugs, and the majority had also experienced mood or anxiety problems. About a third had some kind of personality disorder.

More than a third of these alcohol dependents had fully-recovered from it, around half of them by drinking no alcohol and half by drinking at a low level. Low-risk drinking was taken to mean someone drinks no more than the equivalent of one-and-a-half large beers at a sitting and no more than four large beers a week. Only one-in-six of the people who recovered had treatment. A quarter of the total had remained alcohol dependent and a third were in partial remission, showing some symptoms of alcohol abuse or dependence. Around one-in-six were over their dependency but risking a return to it, drinking the equivalent of more than seven large beers a week or more than two-and-a-half pints on a single day.

These "risky" recovered drinkers were the least likely to have had treatment.

The researchers did a follow-up survey to find out how these same people were getting on three years later.[240] Follow up results showed that risky drinking is deserving of the name. Half of the recovered dependent drinkers who engaged in risky drinking had become dependent again, compared to a quarter of the low-risk drinkers. Younger people were found to be the most likely to return to dependence. The most stable cases of recovery, by a factor of nearly four times, were total abstainers, of whom only 7 per cent had become dependent again.

For all the success of doing it unaided, help delivers some results too. The quarter of US alcohol dependents who look for help are twice as successful in recovering as their counterparts.[241] Their abstinent recovery was four times more likely, while non-abstinent recovery was 50 per cent more likely. Those who also enrolled in a semi-spiritual 12-step programme, like Alcoholics Anonymous, had almost twice the chance of recovery than those who received only medical treatment. There is a possibility, however, that the statistics are skewed because the success of treatment or counselling could be because people who take it are more committed to quitting to begin with.

Life events also contribute to the success or failure of bid to be break free from dependence[242]. Both getting married and getting divorced for the first time increased Americans' chances of moving from alcohol dependency to low-risk drinking in the three years after. After that, chances of pulling-off non-abstinent recovery fall again. The chances of non-abstinent recovery more than doubled among people with children.

Just as alcohol affects people differently, coming off it does too. It is a subjective experience, but there are some general patterns we tend to flow from quitting.[243] Initially, there is an acute withdrawal period of a few days which can manifest itself in sweating, nausea, hyperexcitability, tremors, delirium, and seizures. Any more dramatic symptoms may need to be controlled by a doctor using sedation. Seizures, if they happen, generally to occur in the first two days, peaking at the end of the first. The acute withdrawal period is usually over in a week.

It is then typical to feel anxious and depressed for about six weeks, with women often finding this period is a bit longer. It is likely too that our sleep will be disturbed. After six weeks, we still typically experience elevated anxiety and unease, although at a lower level. People often feel their emotions are "not working normally". They might also complain that things which should make them feel happy do not, a joyless state called *anhedonia*. Seemingly insignificant challenges in our lives can suddenly make us feel desperate, start to crave alcohol, and relapse. Having a lower positive and higher negative expectation of resuming alcohol drinking is a help in continuing our abstinence.[244] We can still feel emotionally unstable for a year or more.

So, recovery from dependence takes quite a long time. After three weeks we might be over the worst of our cravings, but still perform as badly at the Trail-making test as we did when we first quit began.[245] The Trail-making test is a measure of search speed, scanning, processing speed and, mental flexibility, and executive functions.

Recovering dependents also struggle with response inhibition too. They can often get it wrong when, for example, asked to name the colour of the word for a colour is printed in. We might also tend to favour short-term rewards over long-term gains. Another study of abstinent alcoholics found that their balance and gait had improved, but they still had problems with balance with the eyes shut.[246] Sleep can also remain disturbed in long-term alcoholics, with increase in REM and drowsy sleep and less slow-wave sleep.

This combination of frustrating deficiencies likely makes newly-sobered up people more likely to turn back to alcohol. The temptation might be even stronger if we are unaware we have these weaknesses to begin with. It seems likely that this is often the case. Research is patchy, but it appears that something like six months is a realistic timeframe to expect substantial recovery in cognitive functions.[247] Full recovery may take a year or more, and there may be a few niggles still.

This is likely to be a disappointment for those who might be hoping they can quickly detox and move on. But it is also helpful to know what is needed to achieve a goal. There is evidence that cognitive remediation therapy, which aims to improve drinker's cognitive deficits in attention, memory, and executive function can be effective.[248] The results, however, are somewhat tentative.[249]

Physical exercise might also help.[250] It might at least provide an alternative way to relieve anxiety and improve our mood.

Both non-abstinent and abstinent recovery from alcohol dependence are associated with equally significant rises in quality of life.[251] But there seems to be relatively little improvement to be had from curbing heavy, non-dependent drinking. The benefit of cutting down here may be less in the immediate payoff and more in avoiding the risk of pushing our brains over the brink into dependency, when our quality of life takes a sudden nosedive.

We are quite simple creatures, not good at changing habits in the face of unseen risk for slightly obscure, long-term benefits. And giving up drinking is not the quick cure-all we might hope it to be. But it is a starting point for improvement. The fact that we may continue to suffer mood and anxiety problems for a year or more after giving up is a good reason to try to avoid it.[252]

There are two common paths to recovery from alcohol dependency: one relatively spontaneous, coming from changes in our lives; and another which involves a conscious effort to change.[253]

In a study of 38 people who had given up alcohol without treatment all but two had made a decision to give up[254]. The most significant reason was feeling they had too much to lose if they carried on drinking, such as rebuilding trust in relationships and guarding against imminent danger of drink-related health problems. Another common thread in the survey were intrusive fears. Many reported that their success in curbing their drinking came partly thanks to avoiding situations where they might drink and the support of loved ones. Some said it helped to keep mementos of low points, with leaving hole they had punched in a wall. Another, less obtrusively, kept a diary.

The upsides interviewees noted from not drinking were: clearer thinking, improved memory, a greater awareness of surroundings and personal behaviour, and greater insight into emotional states which once caused them distress. "I was always depressed when I was boozing ... now when I get down, I know it will pass," said one of the interviewees, who had been sober for 11 years. Edginess also tended to abate, but some reported problems getting to sleep. Most said their lives had improved, having greater energy and better social relations, including involvement with children.

Some, despite having started drinking to overcome shyness said they had become more outgoing since they stopped. The timescales of recovery, or at least perceived recovery, were again long. One said it took "two or three years to 'straighten out'". It could be that some had actually stopped because they "matured out" of alcohol drinking rather than through a conscious decision to quit. Nevertheless, their decisions related to drinking changed. In all cases, it was common for those taking part in the study to take great pride in their achievement. Someone is, surely, entitled to be pleased to have stopped punching holes in their walls.

There are efforts to make the bumpy road to independence from alcohol smoother and by-the-by make profits for drug companies.[255] In the US, there are three approved drugs to ease the problem, Naltrexone (ReVia, Vivitrol), Acamprosate (Campral) and Disulfiram (Antabuse). The first two attempt to quell cravings and reduce the intoxicating effect of alcohol. Disulfiram, meanwhile, makes alcohol actively unpleasant, making you ill for half-an-hour or so after a glass of wine. An anti-seizure drug called Topiramate has also been found to control impulsivity and there are indications it might help treat alcohol dependence. Researchers are investigating a muscle relaxant and antispasmodic called Baclofen, which may help maintain abstinence.

Some possible leads for future treatments include the finding that formerly alcohol-dependent rats injected with Neuropeptide Y (NPY), a brain chemical regulating emotions, were less likely to seek alcohol when experimenters stressed them out.[256] And Oxytocin, the "cuddle-chemical" associated with sexual behaviour and social bonding, appears to block alcohol's sedative effects in all but the most extreme amounts.[257] An alcohol antidote drug, called Ro15-4513, may have similar promise[258]. There are perhaps dozens more "silver bullets" under investigation.

Drugs may help smooth the path. So too should more widespread knowledge of the effects of alcohol and dependency, as well as what benefits to expect from recovery, and when. ■

# Pursuing happiness

For pioneering American publisher, founding father, diplomat and bon viveur Benjamin Franklin the case for alcohol was quite simple. "Behold the rain which descends from heaven upon our vineyards," he wrote in a letter in 1797, "there it enters the roots of the vines, to be changed into wine, a constant proof that God loves us, and loves to see us happy."

So, alcohol makes us happy, he suggests. It is an extremely appealing thought shared by many of us at times, but wrongly. Alcohol may help achieve other things, like popularity, influence, novelty, excitement, and adventure, perhaps, but not happiness. That is, if we take happiness to be state of mind in which people say they are happy. A lifestyle more like that of a carefree and active parson is more likely to produce a state of self-reported happiness than the hardcore party-hopper.

Epicurus, an ancient Greek who inspired a movement which devoted itself to achieving happiness three hundred years before Jesus Christ, was well ahead of the curve on this. He shunned alcohol and general debauchery as a way to achieving his movement's goal. His approach was not to party hard, but to try to live a wholesome and just life, avoiding harm to others and cultivating friendship. The fundamentals of his approach still seem to deliver results when we try it today.

One of the common problems we have in achieving happiness is that we often do not know what it is. "Chronically happy" people, as they are called in the literature, are not constantly giddy, buoyed-up, chipper, chuffed, or euphoric. Chronically happy people experience a far wider range of feelings, having downs as well as ups, though all interspersed with occasional positive feelings. Happy people may feel upbeat often, but euphoria is not a stepping-stone to achieving happiness.

Instead, happy people seem to get their buzz from their feelings of social connection, belonging, and a confidence in their own resilience.[259] Alcohol consumption, then, by allowing us to feel like we can be more sociable, may very well bring some of the symptoms of chronic happiness. But it can also mean we can blunder, being inconsiderate or clumsy, so weakening the social connections underpinning our happiness. Alcohol causes both happy and unhappy errors.

Hangovers, alcohol-fuelled anxiety and depression, or the withdrawal typical of dependence can also make us feel "delicate" when a feelings of resilience are what help people feel happy. This mean that drinking heavily is likely to make us feel happy less of the time. Alcohol loans us euphoria, charging us interest for it later. We may start to decide we should use alcohol to repay the bill, but the balance may only finally be settled by going without it for an extended period.

Those of us who enjoy a drink tend to feel grateful for alcohol much as Franklin did. And Franklin evidently took the quest for happiness seriously. He signed the US constitution—the work of self-confessed Epicurean Thomas Jefferson—which gives citizens the "inalienable right" to seek it. Franklin may then have opposed America's prohibition of alcohol between 1920 and 1933 as unconstitutional. But the failure of prohibition was not in denying Americans a source of happiness, but the right to pursue it in what seems to be the wrong place.

Research suggests inebriation tends to backfire and have a negative effect on our happiness levels. But it is hard to recognise the disadvantageous trade off, because drinking and feelings of social connection tend to come as a package and the costs of it are delayed by a matter of hours or days.

It may seem unbelievable that we might be drawn to alcohol to satisfy our social craving. Surely there is something more concrete to explain its magnetism? Well, it can after long or intense use change our brains to malfunction without it which can make it alluring by itself.

But we only need to look at the runaway success of social media to see how a social enabler can also be massively compelling without any psychoactive effect or dependence. The daddy of them all, Facebook, now has around 1.5 billion users, while LinkedIn has 400m and Twitter 300m. Even Google+, once the social media choice of the committed hermit, has around 100m. There is no narcotic effect, but we find it hard to control our urge connect with each other on these platforms. Some have taken to calling Facebook "Crackbook" for this reason. We can sometimes prod our mobile phones and flip between browser-tabs like our lives depended on it. This is perhaps because we evolved to live in social units whose acceptance sometimes did mean life or death.

Alcohol feeds our social drive in a similar way, because we see it as a way of connecting with people. And, like social media it offers a level of "deniability" for our mistakes, as politicians might put it. It is possible to say and do rash or silly things when having a drink which we wouldn't at a drink-free occasion. It is okay to be a little foolish. In the same way, it is okay to be brash and clown-around on social media in ways which would raise eyebrows in real life. This freedom is largely result of the extra wiggle-room we offer each other when we drink together, not from alcohol itself. The downsides of the extra scope are similar too. Alcohol, like social media, allows us a means of scaling-up our mistakes as well as our successes.

Alcohol also opens up the chance to connect with our heroes. Among the most prominent overachiever in the Valhalla of inebriation is Winston Churchill. With a world war victory under his belt, who could ever be concerned heavy drinking might be an impediment to even the greatest success? There are other, more renegade figures too, like Ernest Hemingway, Hunter Thompson, and the seemingly immortal Rolling Stone, Keith Richards. Then there are imaginary characters like Norm from US sitcom *Cheers* or gin-swilling "Hawkeye" Pierce from *M\*A\*S\*H* or James Bond.

Inebriation has come to be a byword for feelings of empathy and kinship, the basis of social bonding. Men are particularly attached to alcohol as a way to kickstart their slumbering social skills. We are so accustomed to feeling a kindred spirit with people after a drink, we can easily extend it to other species too. Who does not feel sympathy for a rat with a hangover or a fruit fly having guidance problems?

Seeing a parallel with social media is a potentially useful way to appreciate the "social pressure to drink" we hear about. People do not always thrust a drink into your hand saying, "Go on, a little one won't hurt." It does happen, but it is not necessarily so pro-active. Instead drinking alcohol could be seen as a social medium we suffer for if we ever decide to log out. Leaving creates a feeling of unfriending and losing connection. It seems silly, but this kind of fracture in our pattern of social connection fires the pain centres in our brains. Being on the sidelines of our tribe was potentially much worse than being at a loose end on Friday night. We might not eat or have shelter.

With alcohol, unlike social media, however, the psychological pain of a feeling of social exclusion can often come alongside the agitation and gloom typical of withdrawal. Both discomforts can, at any moment, be resolved by reconnecting to alcohol, the original social marketing. The viral marketing potential is not lost on brewing industry.

It is hard to avoid a persuasive impression. Push open the door of any busy pub or bar on a

Friday or Saturday night and the jovial hoard should satisfy anyone's vision of good cheer. It is a miracle to behold, given that the same people brought together sober might be expected to avoid eye-contact and fiddle with their mobiles. To say what greets you is not a happy scene is to defy the evidence of our eyes. But this is the case: inebriation can often be pleasurable and make us want more of it, but it is different to happiness. The brain activity of happy people and inebriated people are very different.

The difficulty we can have seeing the difference between inebriated euphoria and happiness is made harder because alcohol is generally part of upbeat occasions. It is part of celebrations of all kinds, parties, get-togethers and commemorations, weddings, new jobs, and weekendings. If a marketing executive wanted to maximise the positive associations, they could not ask for better occasions. Consequently, the alcohol brand is stamped on many of the best times in our lives, regardless of its actual contribution. Alcohol and happiness, then, though different, are also so interwoven as to be nigh-on impossible to separate.

The prickly American-born British temperance campaigner Lady Nancy Astor was among those who have sought to keep inebriation in its place. "One reason why I don't drink is because I wish to know when I am having a good time," she said. Few, however, feel the need to be quite so pernickety about the issue. But it would unfair to confuse hair-splitting with being a killjoy. Taking the trouble to distinguish real sources of happiness from mistaken ones can help us conserve and increase happiness. Heavy drinking is just such a case, tending to reduce the happiness reported by people who do it.

It should not be surprising to anyone that alcohol is not a magic potion, apart from those of us who might suffer from believing so. There is nothing to lose in being wary of a substance which impedes our pursuit happiness. ∎

# References

¹ Global status report on alcohol and health 2014
http://www.who.int/substance_abuse/publications/global_
alcohol_report/msb_gsr_2014_1.pdf?ua=1

² Statistics on Alcohol - England, 2013 [NS]
http://www.hscic.gov.uk/catalogue/PUB10932

3 "Iago: Come, come, good wine is a good familiar
creature, if it be well used. Exclaim no more against it."
Othello, Act 2, Scene 3.

4 Just a drop? Alcohol consumption much higher than
reported in England (2013)
http://www.eurekalert.org/pub_releases/2013-02/ucl-
jad022513.php

5 Psychiatric morbidity among adults living in private
households (2000)
http://www.ons.gov.uk/ons/rel/psychiatric-
morbidity/psychiatric-morbidity-among-adults-living-in-
private-households/2000/psychiatric-morbidity-among-
adults-living-in-private-households.pdf

6 People born after World War II are more likely to binge
drink and develop alcohol disorders
http://www.eurekalert.org/pub_releases/2011-09/cums-
pba091611.php

7 Tackling Harmful Alcohol Use (2015)
http://www.oecd-ilibrary.org/social-issues-migration-
health/tackling-harmful-alcohol-use/social-disparities-in-

alcohol-drinking_9789264181069-6-
en;jsessionid=6paqmthft3hka.x-oecd-live-03

8 http://www.ias.org.uk/Alcohol-knowledge-
centre/Economic-
impacts/Factsheets/Economic-benefits.aspx
http://www.statista.com/topics/1709/alcoholic-beverages/

9 Medicinal Brandy (2011)
http://www.ncbi.nlm.nih.gov/pmc/articles/PMC3117141/#b
ib0040

10 Warburg's tincture
http://en.wikipedia.org/wiki/Warburg%27s_tincture#Prope
rties_.2F_formula

11 Drink: A Cultural History of Alcohol (2009)
http://www.amazon.com/Drink-A-Cultural-History-
Alcohol/dp/1592404642


12 Prescribing alcohol in a general hospital: 'Not
everything in black and white makes sense' (1998)
http://www.ncbi.nlm.nih.gov/pubmed/9762632

13 Alcohol and Cardiovascular Health: The Razor-Sharp
Double-Edged Sword (2007)
http://www.sciencedirect.com/science/article/pii/S0735109
7070200

14 Wine, beer or spirit drinking in relation to fatal and
non-fatal cardiovascular events: a meta-analysis (2011)
http://www.ncbi.nlm.nih.gov/pubmed/22076059

15 Non-Alcoholic Red Wine May Boost Heart Health
(2012)
http://www.webmd.com/hypertension-high-blood-
pressure/news/20120906/nonalcoholic-red-wine-may-
boost-heart-health

16 Nonalcoholic beverages may impart cardiovascular
benefits without the negative effects of alcohol (2004)
http://www.eurekalert.org/pub_releases/2004-05/ace-

nbm050604.php

[17] Gastronomic meal of the French (2010)
http://www.unesco.org/culture/ich/index.php?lg=en&pg=0
0011&RL=00437

[18] Mediterranean diet (2013)
http://www.unesco.org/culture/ich/index.php?lg=en&pg=0
0011&RL=00884

[19] Effects of Wine, Alcohol and Polyphenols on Cardiovascular Disease Risk Factors (2013)

http://www.medscape.com/viewarticle/803472_4

[20] Alcohol in Moderation, Cardioprotection and Neuroprotection: Epidemiological Considerations and Mechanistic Studies (2009)

http://www.ncbi.nlm.nih.gov/pmc/articles/PMC290837
3/

[21] Irregular heavy drinking occasions and risk of ischemic heart disease: a systematic review and meta-analysis (2010)
http://www.ncbi.nlm.nih.gov/pubmed/20142394

[22] Alcohol and Cardiovascular Health: The Razor-Sharp Double-Edged Sword

https://content.onlinejacc.org/data/Journals/JAC/2309
7/04089.pdf

[23] Tolerance in Drosophila (2009)
http://www.ncbi.nlm.nih.gov/pubmed/19180359

[24] Daily alcohol use causes changes in sexual behavior, new study reveals (2008)
http://www.eurekalert.org/pub_releases/2008-01/ps-
dau122707.php

[25] Fermenting fruit and the historical ecology of ethanol ingestion: is alcoholism in modern humans an evolutionary hangover? (2002)
http://www.ncbi.nlm.nih.gov/pubmed/11964055

[26] New strain of lab mice mimics human alcohol

consumption patterns (2011)
http://www.eurekalert.org/pub_releases/2011-12/iuui-ns121211.php

[27] "The Beautiful and Damned", F Scott Fitzgerald (1922)

[28] Patterns of alcohol expectancies and alcohol use across age and gender (2012)
http://www.ncbi.nlm.nih.gov/pubmed/22748519

[29] Cheers? Understanding the relationship between alcohol and mental health (2006)
http://www.mentalhealth.org.uk/content/assets/PDF/publications/cheers_report.pdf?view=Standard

[30] Alcohol in Europe A public health perspective (2006)
http://ec.europa.eu/health/archive/ph_determinants/life_style/alcohol/documents/alcohol_europe_en.pdf

[31] Stress and alcohol 'feed' each other (2011)
http://www.eurekalert.org/pub_releases/2011-07/ace-saa070711.php

[32] Alcohol Outcome Expectancies as Socially Shared and Socialized Beliefs (2009)
http://www.ncbi.nlm.nih.gov/pmc/articles/PMC2709745/

[33] Alcohol expectancies in young children and how this relates to parental alcohol use (2015)
http://www.ncbi.nlm.nih.gov/pubmed/25655929

[34] Early drinking in teens linked to alcohol use in movies (2006)
http://www.eurekalert.org/pub_releases/2006-01/dms-edio11206.php

[35] Underage drinkers account for about 17 per cent of consumer expenditures for alcohol (2006)
http://www.eurekalert.org/pub_releases/2006-05/jaaj-uda042706.php

[36] Alcohol Outcome Expectancies as Socially Shared and Socialized Beliefs (2009)

http://www.ncbi.nlm.nih.gov/pmc/articles/PMC2709745/

37 Teenage alcohol and drug use: At best, parents know about it only half of the time (2006)
http://www.eurekalert.org/pub_releases/2006-09/ace-taa091706.php

38 Children are introduced to sipping and tasting alcohol in the home
http://www.eurekalert.org/pub_releases/2008-01/ace-cai122807.php

39 Both gender and friendship can influence adolescent alcohol use (2007)
http://www.eurekalert.org/pub_releases/2007-11/ace-bga111907.php

40 Linking masculinity to negative drinking consequences: the mediating roles of heavy episodic drinking and alcohol expectancies (2014)
http://www.ncbi.nlm.nih.gov/pubmed/24766763

[41] Life course trajectories of alcohol consumption in the United Kingdom using longitudinal data from nine cohort studies (2015)
http://www.biomedcentral.com/content/pdf/s12916-015-0273-z.pdf

[42] Drinking buddies and their prospective influence on alcohol outcomes: Alcohol expectancies as a mediator (2013)
http://www.ncbi.nlm.nih.gov/pmc/articles/PMC3588170/

43 Alcohol Expectancy Challenges: A Comprehensive Review
http://www.sbm.org/meeting/2010/presentations/Saturday/Paper%20Session%2031/Alcohol%20Expectancy%20Challenges%20A%20Comprehensive%20Review.pdf

44 A Prospective Study of Alcohol Expectancies and Self-Efficacy as Predictors of Young Adolescent Alcohol Misuse
http://alcalc.oxfordjournals.org/content/46/2/161

45 The relationship between parental alcohol use and college students' alcohol-related cognitions (2013)
http://www.ncbi.nlm.nih.gov/pubmed/23954562

46 Alcohol expectancy changes over a 12-week cognitive-behavioral therapy program are predictive of treatment success (2011)
http://www.ncbi.nlm.nih.gov/pubmed/2086429

47 The Anticipated Effects of Alcohol Scale: Development and Psychometric Evaluation of a Novel Assessment Tool for Measuring Alcohol Expectancies (2014)
http://www.ncbi.nlm.nih.gov/pmc/articles/PMC3915927/

48 Loss of control drinking in alcoholics: an experimental analogue (1973)
http://www.ncbi.nlm.nih.gov/pubmed/4710045

49 The effects of alcohol, expectancy, and alcohol beliefs on anxiety and self-disclosure in women: do beliefs moderate alcohol effects? (1994)
http://www.ncbi.nlm.nih.gov/pubmed/7832009

50 The effects of alcohol expectancy priming on group bonding (2013)
http://www.ncbi.nlm.nih.gov/pubmed/24128149

51 Drinking experience uncovers genetic influences on alcohol expectancies across adolescence (2015)
http://onlinelibrary.wiley.com/doi/10.1111/add.12845/abstract

52 Alcohol expectancies in childhood: change with the onset of drinking and ability to predict adolescent drunkenness and binge drinking (2015)
http://europepmc.org/abstract/MED/25117029

53 Response to alcohol, peers, expectancies, and coping all contribute to adolescent drinking (2011)
http://www.eurekalert.org/pub_releases/2011-07/ace-rta070711.php

54 Teens who drink alone more likely to develop alcohol problems as young adults

http://www.eurekalert.org/pub_releases/2013-11/cmu-twd111813.php

55 Alcohol-dependent patients have weak negative rather than strong positive implicit alcohol associations (2013)http://www.ncbi.nlm.nih.gov/pmc/articles/PMC3726926/

56 Understanding Alcohol Expectancy Effects: Revisiting the Placebo Condition (2006)

http://www.ncbi.nlm.nih.gov/pmc/articles/PMC1403295/

57 Alcohol-related Deaths in the United Kingdom, Registered in 2013
http://www.ons.gov.uk/ons/rel/subnational-health4/alcohol-related-deaths-in-the-united-kingdom/2012/sty-alcohol-releated-deaths.html

58 Liver disease biggest cause of alcohol-related deaths in England and Wales
http://www.ons.gov.uk/ons/rel/subnational-health4/alcohol-related-deaths-in-the-united-kingdom/2012/sty-alcohol-releated-deaths.html

[59] Overview: How Is Alcohol Metabolized by the Body?

http://pubs.niaaa.nih.gov/publications/arh294/245-255.htm

[60] Salsolinol modulation of dopamine neurons (2013)

http://www.ncbi.nlm.nih.gov/pubmed/23745110

[61] Short-term effects of alcohol

http://en.wikipedia.org/wiki/Short-term_effects_of_alcohol

[62] Alcohol banned from rifle competitions

http://www.dailynebraskan.com/sports/alcohol-banned-from-rifle-competitions/article_208d46e3-8e6f-54b4-a2d5-

98aef12ab40e.html

[63] Drunk' fruit flies could shed light on genetic basis of human alcohol abuse
http://www.eurekalert.org/pub_releases/2006-10/bc-ff101606.php

[64] Infant rats eagerly accept high concentrations of alcohol upon first exposure (2004)
http://www.eurekalert.org/pub_releases/2004-08/ace-ireo80504.php

[65] Teens who drink with parents may still develop alcohol problems (2010)
http://www.eurekalert.org/pub_releases/2010-01/joso-twd012710.php

[66] 30% of Children Scared by Adults' Drinking (2010)
http://www.ias.org.uk/News/Older/05-July-2010-30-of-Children-Scared-by-Adults-Drinking.aspx

[67] Early Drinking Linked to Higher Lifetime Alcoholism Risk (2006)
http://www.niaaa.nih.gov/news-events/news-releases/early-drinking-linked-higher-lifetime-alcoholism-risk

[68] Adolescent rats help prove that early alcohol exposure alcohol can quickly lead to heavy drinking (2008)
http://www.eurekalert.org/pub_releases/2008-05/ace-arho42808.php

[69] Age of Drinking Onset Predicts Future Alcohol Abuse and Dependence (1998) http://www.niaaa.nih.gov/news-events/news-releases/age-drinking-onset-predicts-future-alcohol-abuse-and-dependence
http://www.ncbi.nlm.nih.gov/pubmed/9494942

[70] Study Reveals New Genes for Excessive Alcohol Drinking (2006)
http://www.niaaa.nih.gov/news-events/news-

releases/study-reveals-new-genes-excessive-alcohol-drinking

[71]NIH study identifies gene for alcohol preference in rats (2013)

http://www.niaaa.nih.gov/news-events/news-releases/gene-alcohol-preference

[72] Symptoms of alcohol abuse, not dependence, may better reflect family risk for alcohol use disorders

http://www.eurekalert.org/pub_releases/2012-09/ace-soa090712.php

[73] Less intense response to alcohol sheds light on genetic tracing of alcohol dependence (2005)
http://www.eurekalert.org/pub_releases/2005-07/ama-liro71405.php

[74] Fruit Fly Study Identifies Gene Mutation That Regulates Sensitivity to Alcohol (2006)

http://www.niaaa.nih.gov/news-events/news-releases/fruit-fly-study-identifies-gene-mutation-regulates-sensitivity-alcohol

[75] Researchers find an association between alcohol dependence and the GABAA receptor gene GABRG3 (2004) http://www.eurekalert.org/pub_releases/2004-01/ace-rfa010704.php

[76] Cannabinoid receptor 1 is linked to dependence on alcohol and other substances (2011)
http://www.eurekalert.org/pub_releases/2011-11/ace-cr1110811.php

[77] Effects of alcohol in young binge drinkers predicts future alcoholism (2014)
http://www.eurekalert.org/pub_releases/2014-05/uocm-eoa051514.php

[78] Sensitivity to alcohol odors may indicate a genetic predisposition to alcohol dependence (2010)

http://www.eurekalert.org/pub_releases/2010-09/ace-sta090110.php

[79] Same Genes May Underlie Alcohol and Nicotine Co-Abuse (2006)
http://www.niaaa.nih.gov/news-events/news-releases/same-genes-may-underlie-alcohol-and-nicotine-co-abuse

[80] Increased Attributable Risk Related to a Functional m-Opioid Receptor Gene Polymorphism in Association with Alcohol Dependence in Central Sweden (2005)
http://www (2014)
.nature.com/npp/journal/v30/n2/pdf/1300598a.pdf?origin=publication_detail

http://www.nih.gov/news/pr/mar2007/niaaa-06.htm

http://www.nih.gov/news/health/may2010/niaaa-18.htm

http://www.niaaa.nih.gov/news-events/news-releases/receptor-variant-influences-dopamine-response-alcoho

[81] The mu opioid receptor genotype may be a marker for those who drink for alcohol's rewarding effects (2012)

[82] Receptor Variant Influences Dopamine Response to Alcohol (2010)
http://www.nih.gov/news/health/may2010/niaaa-18.htm

[83] Brain dopamine may serve as a risk marker for alcohol use disorders (2013)
http://www.eurekalert.org/pub_releases/2013-08/ace-bdm080213.php

[84] The G allele of the mu-opioid receptor gene is linked to craving for alcohol (2007)
http://www.eurekalert.org/pub_releases/2007-01/ace-tga122706.php

[85] A genetic difference at the opiate receptor gene affects

a person's response to alcohol (2004)
http://www.eurekalert.org/pub_releases/2004-12/ace-agd120504.php

[86] The mu opioid receptor genotype may be a marker for those who drink for alcohol's rewarding effects (2012)
http://www.eurekalert.org/pub_releases/2012-12/ace-tmo120712.php

[87] Serotonin Transporter Gene Shown to Influence College Drinking Habits (2003) Journal of Alcohol and Alcoholism http://www.niaaa.nih.gov/news-events/news-releases/study-reveals-new-genes-excessive-alcohol-drinking

[88] The course of anxiety, depression and drinking behaviours after completed detoxification in alcoholics with and without comorbid anxiety and depressive disorders (2001)
http://www.ncbi.nlm.nih.gov/pubmed/11373263

[89] NIH study finds chronic alcohol use shifts brain's control of behavior (2013)
http://www.niaaa.nih.gov/news-events/news-releases/chronic-alcohol-use-shifts-behavior-control

[90] Self-reported life satisfaction and alcohol use: a 15-year follow-up of healthy adult twins
http://www.ncbi.nlm.nih.gov/pubmed/22215005

[91] Heavy drinking occasions and depression (2006)
http://www.ncbi.nlm.nih.gov/pubmed/16490791

[92] Alcohol-Related Psychosis
http://misc.medscape.com/pi/iphone/medscapeapp/html/A289848-business.html

[93] Chronic Drinking May Alter Brain to Increase PTSD Risk (2012)
http://www.niaaa.nih.gov/research/niaaa-research-highlights/chronic-drinking-may-alter-brain-increase-ptsd-risk

[94] Scientists Link Chromatin Modifications with Alcohol Withdrawal Anxiety (2008)
http://www.niaaa.nih.gov/news-events/news-releases/scientists-link-chromatin-modifications-alcohol-withdrawal-anxiety

[95] Study Links Receptor to Stress-Induced Alcohol Relapse (2006)
http://www.nih.gov/news/pr/oct2006/niaaa-02.htm

[96] What roles do mesolimbic and neostriatal dopamine systems play in reward? (1998)
http://www.ncbi.nlm.nih.gov/pubmed/9858756

[97] Alcohol helps the brain remember, says new study (2011) http://www.eurekalert.org/pub_releases/2011-04/uota-aht041211.php

[98] Biography of George Jean Nathan
http://english.arts.cornell.edu/awards/nathan/bio.html

[99] Alcohol myopia and goal commitment (2014)
http://www.ncbi.nlm.nih.gov/pmc/articles/PMC3941585/

[100] Encoding-imagery specificity in alcohol state-dependent learning (1976)
http://www.ncbi.nlm.nih.gov/pubmed/1249533

[101] Alcohol myopia: Its prized and dangerous effects (1990)
http://han.uni-graz.at/han/28980/ovidsp.tx.ovid.com/sp-3.14.0b/ovidweb.cgi?&S=IPGIFPOMEJDDPAAPNCLKMHGCFEJHAA00&Link+Set=jb.search.28%7c1%7csl_10

[102] Smoking reduces alcohol's effects, likely encouraging more drinking
http://www.eurekalert.org/pub_releases/2006-07/ace-sra071706.php

[103] Insight into alcohol-nicotine interaction might lead to new quitting method (2004)

http://www.eurekalert.org/pub_releases/2004-03/dumc-iia032204.php

[104] The Influence of Alcohol Intake and Alcohol Expectations on the Recognition of Emotions (2011)
http://alcalc.oxfordjournals.org/content/46/6/680

[105] The biology behind alcohol-induced blackouts

http://www.eurekalert.org/pub_releases/2011-07/wuso-tbb070611.php

[106] Alcohol can lead to unsafe sex: It's official (2011)
http://www.eurekalert.org/pub_releases/2011-12/w-acl120811.php

[107] Differential Effects of Alcohol on Working Memory: Distinguishing Multiple Processes (2007)
http://www.ncbi.nlm.nih.gov/pmc/articles/PMC2658822/

[108] Alcohol Affects Emotion Through Cognition (2001)
http://han.uni-graz.at/han/16890/web.a.ebscohost.com/ehost/detail/detail?sid=d2be8506-d409-430d-be6d-4ae872e6017b%40sessionmgr4005&vid=0&hid=4214&bdata=JnNpdGU9ZWhvc3QtbGl2ZQ%3d%3d#db=buh&AN=5408286

[109] Are You Insulting Me? Exposure to Alcohol Primes Increases Aggression Following Ambiguous Provocation (2015)

http://psp.sagepub.com/content/40/8/1037

[110] Alcohol makes smiles more 'contagious,' but only for men (2014)
http://www.sciencedaily.com/releases/2014/09/140930090634.htm

[111] Alcohol dulls brain 'alarm' that monitors mistakes, MU study finds (2011)
http://www.eurekalert.org/pub_releases/2011-09/uom-adb090111.php

[112]Alcohol increases reaction time and errors during

decision making (2010)
http://www.eurekalert.org/pub_releases/2010-10/ace-air101210.php

[113] Racial stereotyping increases after being exposed to alcohol-related images says MU psychologist (2012)

http://www.eurekalert.org/pub_releases/2012-03/uom-rsi032712.php

[114] Not all forms of anger lead to alcohol-related aggression (2003)
http://www.eurekalert.org/pub_releases/2003-12/ace-naf120703.php

[115] Cognitive Processes in Alcohol Binges: A Review and Research Agenda 2008

http://www.ncbi.nlm.nih.gov/pmc/articles/PMC3066447/

[116] https://www.ncadd.org/about-addiction/alcohol-drugs-and-crime

[117] The Effects of Acute Alcohol Consumption, Cognitive Reserve, Partner Risk, and Gender on Sexual Decision Making (2006)

http://www.ncbi.nlm.nih.gov/pmc/articles/PMC4477198/

[118] The effects of acute alcohol consumption, cognitive reserve, partner risk, and gender on sexual decision making.

http://www.ncbi.nlm.nih.gov/pubmed/16536135

[119] Effects of Acute Alcohol Consumption on Ratings of Attractiveness of Facial Stimuli (2008)

http://alcalc.oxfordjournals.org/content/43/6/636

[120] The Moderating Effect of Stimulus Attractiveness on the Effect of Alcohol Consumption on Attractiveness Ratings

http://www.ncbi.nlm.nih.gov/pubmed/24858916

[121] Drinking small amounts of alcohol boosts people's

sense of smell (2014)
http://digest.bps.org.uk/2014/08/drinking-small-amounts-of-alcohol.html

[122] Lost in the Sauce The Effects of Alcohol on Mind Wandering? (2009)
http://www.ncbi.nlm.nih.gov/pmc/articles/PMC2724753/

[123] More than half of Dry January pledges have already fallen off the wagon (Independent, January 22nd 2015)
http://www.independent.co.uk/life-style/health-and-families/more-than-half-of-dry-january-pledges-have-already-fallen-off-the-wagon-9994486.html

[124] Boosting slow oscillations during sleep potentiates memory (2006)
http://www.nature.com/nature/journal/v444/n7119/full/nature05278.html

[125] http://en.wikipedia.org/wiki/Slow-wave_sleep#Discussion

[126] Alcohol's disruptive effects on sleep may be more pronounced among women
http://www.eurekalert.org/pub_releases/2011-02/ace-ade020811.php

[127] Alcohol and sleep I: effects on normal sleep (2013)
http://www.ncbi.nlm.nih.gov/pubmed/23347102

[128]The acute effects of alcohol on sleep architecture in late adolescence (2013)
http://www.ncbi.nlm.nih.gov/pubmed/23800287

[129] Rapid tolerance development to the NREM sleep promoting effect of alcohol (2014)
http://www.ncbi.nlm.nih.gov/pubmed/24899768

[130] The Acute Effects of Alcohol on Sleep Electroencephalogram Power Spectra in Late Adolescence (2015)
http://www.ncbi.nlm.nih.gov/pubmed/25597245

[131]The acute effects of alcohol on sleep architecture in late

adolescence (2013)

http://www.ncbi.nlm.nih.gov/pubmed/23800287

[132]Prevalence and Correlates of Alpha-Delta Sleep in Major Depressive Disorders (2011)

http://www.ncbi.nlm.nih.gov/pmc/articles/PMC3159543

[133] Alcohol interferes with the restorative functions of sleep (2011)

http://www.eurekalert.org/pub_releases/2011-08/ace-aiw080811.php

[134] Acute binge alcohol administration reverses sleep-wake cycle in sprague dawley rats (2014)

http://www.ncbi.nlm.nih.gov/pubmed/24930893

[135]Sleep-wakefulness in alcohol preferring and non-preferring rats following binge alcohol administration.

http://www.ncbi.nlm.nih.gov/pubmed/20621165

[136] Habitual moderate alcohol consumption desynchronizes circadian physiologic rhythms and affects reaction-time performance (2010)

http://www.ncbi.nlm.nih.gov/pubmed/20969532

[137] Ingestion of ethanol just prior to sleep onset impairs memory for procedural but not declarative tasks (2003)

http://www.ncbi.nlm.nih.gov/pubmed/12683478

[138] Alcohol and Sleep Restriction Combined Reduces Vigilant Attention, Whereas Sleep Restriction Alone Enhances Distractibility (2014)

http://www.ncbi.nlm.nih.gov/pubmed/25515101

[139] Alcohol hangover: type and time-extension of motor function impairments (2013)

http://www.ncbi.nlm.nih.gov/pubmed/23557691

[140] Alterations in affective behavior during the time course of alcohol hangover (2013)

http://www.ncbi.nlm.nih.gov/pubmed/25023858

[141] Brain reward deficits accompany withdrawal

(hangover) from acute ethanol in rats (2006)

http://www.ncbi.nlm.nih.gov/pubmed/16938626

[142] Drunken worms reveal a genetic basis of alcohol response (2004)

http://www.eurekalert.org/pub_releases/2004-06/cp-dwr060304.php

[143] A Review of the Next Day Effects of Alcohol on Subjective Mood Ratings (2010)

http://www.ncbi.nlm.nih.gov/pubmed/20712597

[144] Measurement of alcohol hangover severity: development of the Alcohol Hangover Severity Scale (AHSS).

http://www.ncbi.nlm.nih.gov/pubmed/23007602

[145] Hangover research needs: proceedings of the 5th Alcohol Hangover Research Group meeting (2013)

http://www.ncbi.nlm.nih.gov/pubmed/24444044

[146] Alcohol hangover: a critical review of explanatory factors (2009)

http://www.ncbi.nlm.nih.gov/pubmed/19347842

[147] Genetic influences on alcohol-related hangover (2014)
http://www.ncbi.nlm.nih.gov/pubmed/25098862

[148] The pathology of alcohol hangover (2010)

http://www.ncbi.nlm.nih.gov/pubmed/20712596

[149] Acute withdrawal: diagnosis and treatment (2014)
http://www.ncbi.nlm.nih.gov/pubmed/25307572

[150] Alcohol hangover: a critical review of explanatory factors (2009)

http://www.ncbi.nlm.nih.gov/pubmed/19347842

[151] Alcohol hangover symptoms and their contribution to the overall hangover severity (2012)

http://www.ncbi.nlm.nih.gov/pubmed/22434663

[152] A review of the literature on the cognitive effects of alcohol hangover (2008)

http://www.ncbi.nlm.nih.gov/pubmed/18238851

[153] A critical analysis of alcohol hangover research methodology for surveys or studies of effects on cognition.(2014)

http://www.ncbi.nlm.nih.gov/pubmed/24633471

[154] Effects of alcohol hangover on simulated highway driving performance.

http://www.ncbi.nlm.nih.gov/pubmed/24563184

[155] Alcohol hangover as a cause of impairment in apprehended drivers (2015)

http://www.ncbi.nlm.nih.gov/pubmed/25023858

[156] Direct comparison of the cognitive effects of acute alcohol with the morning after a normal night's drinking.

http://www.ncbi.nlm.nih.gov/pubmed/22499407

[157] The pathology of alcohol hangover (2010)

http://www.ncbi.nlm.nih.gov/pubmed/20712596

[158] Heritability of usual alcohol intoxication and hangover in male twins: the NAS-NRC twin registry.(2014)

http://www.ncbi.nlm.nih.gov/pubmed/25156618

[159] Alcohol hangover: a critical review of explanatory factors (2009)

http://www.ncbi.nlm.nih.gov/pubmed/19347842

[160] Alterations of motor performance and brain cortex mitochondrial function during ethanol hangover (2012) http://www.ncbi.nlm.nih.gov/pubmed/22608205

[161] Alcohol interferes with the restorative functions of sleep (2011)

http://www.eurekalert.org/pub_releases/2011-08/ace-aiwo80811.php

[162] The effect of constant darkness and circadian resynchronization on the recovery of alcohol hangover (2014)

http://www.ncbi.nlm.nih.gov/pubmed/24717330

[163] Age of Onset and Temporal Sequencing of Lifetime

DSM-IV Alcohol Use Disorders Relative to Comorbid Mood and Anxiety Disorders* (2009)
http://www.ncbi.nlm.nih.gov/pmc/articles/PMC2386955/

[164] Global status report on alcohol and health (2014)
http://apps.who.int/iris/bitstream/10665/112736/1/978
9240692763_eng.pdf?ua=1

[165] Alcohol abusers' depression often related to drinking (2013)
http://www.eurekalert.org/pub_releases/2013-02/joso-aad020713.php

[166] Comparative Quantification of Health Risks, Global and Regional Burden of Disease Attributable to Selected Major Risk Factors, Volume 1 (2004)
http://www.who.int/publications/cra/chapters/volume1/09
59-1108.pdf

[167] Comparative Quantification of Health Risks, Global and Regional Burden of Disease Attributable to Selected Major Risk Factors, Volume 1 (2004)
http://www.who.int/publications/cra/chapters/volume1/09
59-1108.pdf

[168] Prevalence and Co-Occurrence of Substance Use Disorders and Independent Mood and Anxiety Disorders (2004)
http://archpsyc.jamanetwork.com/article.aspx?articleid=48
2045

[169] Chronic alcoholism and male sexual function (1995)
http://ajp.psychiatryonline.org/doi/pdf/10.1176/ajp.152.7.1
045

[170] Stressful life experiences, alcohol consumption, and alcohol use disorders: the epidemiologic evidence for four main types of stressors (2011)
http://www.ncbi.nlm.nih.gov/pmc/articles/PMC3755727/

[171] https://www.drinkaware.co.uk/check-the-facts/health-effects-of-alcohol/mental-health/alcohol-and-

mental-health#depression

[172] Age of Onset and Temporal Sequencing of Lifetime DSM-IV Alcohol Use Disorders Relative to Comorbid Mood and Anxiety Disorders* (2009)
http://www.ncbi.nlm.nih.gov/pmc/articles/PMC2386955/

[173] Anxiety and depression among abstainers and low-level alcohol consumers. The Nord-Trøndelag Health Study (2009)
http://onlinelibrary.wiley.com/doi/10.1111/j.1360-0443.2009.02659.x/abstract

[174] Underage Drinking: A Major Public Health Challenge (2003)
http://pubs.niaaa.nih.gov/publications/aa59.htm

[175] Choose three or more from seven:
$^7C_3 + {^7C_4} + {^7C_5} + {^7C_6} + {^7C_7} = 35 + 35 + 21 + 7 + 1 = 99$

[176] Choose three or four from the four remaining symptoms: $^4C_3 + {^4C_4} = 5$

[177] ICD-10 Version:2015
http://apps.who.int/classifications/icd10/browse/2015/en#

[178] By guessing, clinicians may miss 3/4 of alcohol problems (2013)
http://www.eurekalert.org/pub_releases/2013-02/uoth-bgc021313.php

[179] Smoking indicator of alcohol misuse (2007)
http://www.eurekalert.org/pub_releases/2007-04/yu-sio041807.php

180 How will alcohol sales in the UK be affected if drinkers follow government guidelines? (2009)
http://www.ncbi.nlm.nih.gov/pubmed/19734160

[181] Association of Average Daily Alcohol Consumption, Binge Drinking and Alcohol-Related Social
http://alcalc.oxfordjournals.org/content/44/3/314.abstract

[182] Heavy Alcohol Consumption During Adolescence Compromises Hippocampal Development

http://www.ncbi.nlm.nih.gov/pubmed/20534463

[183] Binge Drinking in Adolescents: A Review of Neurophysiological and Neuroimaging Research

http://alcalc.oxfordjournals.org/content/49/2/198.abstract

[184] Binge Drinking in Adolescents: A Review of Neurophysiological and Neuroimaging Research (2013)

[185] Heavy drinking occasions and depression. (2006) http://www.ncbi.nlm.nih.gov/pubmed/16490791

[186]Cognitive and emotional consequences of binge drinking: role of amygdala and prefrontal cortex http://www.ncbi.nlm.nih.gov/pmc/articles/PMC2607328/~

[187] Inside the brain of an alcoholic http://www.newscientist.com/article/dn8676-inside-the-brain-of-an-alcoholic.html#.VI7eBtLF95c

[188]Acute withdrawal, protracted abstinence and negative affect in alcoholism: Are they linked? http://www.ncbi.nlm.nih.gov/pmc/articles/PMC3268458/

[189] Executive function: primer (2008) http://www.icn.ucl.ac.uk/executive_functions/pubs/gilbert%20burgess%202008%20curr%20biol.pdf

[190] Are executive function and impulsivity antipodes? A conceptual reconstruction with special reference to addiction (2012)

http://www.ncbi.nlm.nih.gov/pubmed/22441659

[191] Effects of heavy drinking on executive cognitive functioning in a community sample (2014) http://www.ncbi.nlm.nih.gov/pubmed/24459697

[192] Cognitive functioning in sober social drinkers: a review of the research since 1986 (1998) http://www.ncbi.nlm.nih.gov/pubmed/9500305

[193] Alcohol damages day-to-day memory function http://www.eurekalert.org/pub_releases/2003-06/ace-

add060903.php

194 The effects of heavy social drinking on executive function: a systematic review and meta-analytic study of existing literature and new empirical findings (2013) http://www.ncbi.nlm.nih.gov/pubmed/22389083

195 Mind Deficit in Subjects with Alcohol Use Disorder: An Analysis of Mindreading Processes (2013) http://alcalc.oxfordjournals.org/content/49/3/299

196Effects of a persistent binge drinking pattern of alcohol consumption in young people: a follow-up study using event-related potentials http://www.ncbi.nlm.nih.gov/pubmed/23695975

197 Brain Structure in Adolescents and Young Adults with Alcohol Problems: Systematic Review of Imaging Studies
http://alcalc.oxfordjournals.org/content/43/2/124.extract

198 Pathways to alcohol-induced brain impairment in young people: A review (2012) http://www.sciencedirect.com/science/article/pii/S001094 5212001839

199 An inverse relationship between typical alcohol consumption and facial symmetry detection ability in young women (2007) http://www.ncbi.nlm.nih.gov/pubmed/17259210

200 Alcohol consumption and frontal lobe shrinkage: study of 1432 non-alcoholic subjects (2001)
http://www.ncbi.nlm.nih.gov/pmc/articles/PMC287234 5/#b76-ijerph-07-01540

201 Ethanol and Cognition: Indirect Effects, Neurotoxicity and Neuroprotection: A Review (2010)
http://www.ncbi.nlm.nih.gov/pmc/articles/PMC287234 5/#b76-ijerph-07-01540

202 http://en.wikipedia.org/wiki/Prefrontal_cortex

[203] Frontal lobe changes in alcholism: a review of the literature (2001)
http://alcalc.oxfordjournals.org/content/36/5/357.abstract

[204] Decreased prefrontal cortical dopamine transmission in alcoholism (2014)
http://www.ncbi.nlm.nih.gov/pubmed/24874293

[205] Biochemical and Neurotransmitter Changes Implicated in Alcohol-Induced Brain Damage in Chronic or 'Binge Drinking' Alcohol Abuse
http://alcalc.oxfordjournals.org/content/44/2/128.abstract

[206] The Wisconsin Card Sorting Test and the cognitive assessment of prefrontal executive functions: A critical update (2009)
https://www.bowdoin.edu/faculty/e/enyhus/pdf/nyhus, barcelo,2009.pdf

[207] Neurocognitive deficits, craving, and abstinence among alcohol-dependent individuals following detoxification (2013)
http://www.ncbi.nlm.nih.gov/pubmed/24334264

[208] Alcohol and the pre-frontal cortex
http://www.ncbi.nlm.nih.gov/pmc/articles/PMC3593065/

[209] The effects of heavy social drinking on executive function: a systematic review and meta-analytic study of existing literature and new empirical findings (2012)
http://www.ncbi.nlm.nih.gov/pubmed/22389083

[210] International Social Survey Programme 1998
http://www.jdsurvey.net/jds/jdsurveyAnalisis.jsp?ES_COL=127&Idioma=I&SeccionCol=05&ESID=500

[211] Alcoholics Anonymous, Fourth Edition, Alcoholics Anonymous World Services, Inc, 2001

[212] Skinner 1972; Crick 1994

[213]Addiction and free will (2009)
http://www.ncbi.nlm.nih.gov/pmc/articles/PMC2757759/

[214] Stillman and Baumeister 2008/unpublished

[215] Stillman and Baumeister 2008/unpublished

[216] Traynor v. Turnage 485 U.S. 535 (1988)
https://supreme.justia.com/cases/federal/us/485/535/case.html

217 Alcohol impairs executive cognitive functioning much longer than expected (2003)
http://www.eurekalert.org/pub_releases/2003-05/ace-aie050703.php

218 Alcohol-Related Aggression—Social and Neurobiological Factors (2013)
http://www.aerzteblatt.de/pdf.asp?id=147679

219 Alcohol-Related Aggression—Social and Neurobiological Factors (2013)
http://www.aerzteblatt.de/pdf.asp?id=147679

220 Alcohol and suicide (1983)
http://www.ncbi.nlm.nih.gov/pubmed/6648755

221 Fears of drink spiking distract from the dangers of alcohol (2009)
http://www.ias.org.uk/News/Older/29-October-2009-Fears-of-drink-spiking-distract-from-the-dangers-of-alcohol.aspx

[222] Chaos theory may help explain patterns of alcohol abuse, studies suggest (2003)
http://www.eurekalert.org/pub_releases/2003-04/osu-ctm041603.php

[223] Global status report on alcohol and health 2014
http://www.who.int/substance_abuse/publications/global_alcohol_report/msb_gsr_2014_1.pdf?ua=1

[224]Toward the attainment of low-risk drinking goals: a 10-year progress report (2004)

http://www.ncbi.nlm.nih.gov/pubmed/15365308

[225] Health Behaviors of Adults: United States, 2005–2007
http://www.cdc.gov/nchs/data/series/sr_10/sr10_245.pdf

[226]Alcohol in Europe: A public health perspective
http://ec.europa.eu/health/archive/ph_determinants/lif
e_style/alcohol/documents/alcohol_europe_en.pdf

[227] Transitions In and Out of Alcohol Use Disorders:
Their Associations with Conditional Changes in Quality of
Life Over a 3-Year Follow-Up Interval (2008)
http://www.ncbi.nlm.nih.gov/pmc/articles/PMC2605522/#
R27

[228] http://en.wikipedia.org/wiki/Alcoholism

[229] Researchers Identify Alcoholism Subtypes (2007)
http://www.niaaa.nih.gov/news-events/news-
releases/researchers-identify-alcoholism-subtypes

[230] Perceived Need for Treatment for Alcohol Use
Disorders: Results from Two National Surveys (2010)
http://www.ncbi.nlm.nih.gov/pmc/articles/PMC285920
1/

[231] Help-seeking and recovery by problem drinkers:
Characteristics of drinkers who attended alcoholics
anonymous or formal treatment or who recovered without
assistance (1993)
http://www.sciencedirect.com/science/article/pii/0306460
39390069L

[232] Interventions for alcohol dependence in Europe: a
missed opportunity to improve public health (May 2012)
http://www.uems.eu/__data/assets/pdf_file/0011/1550/Su
mmary_Report_Interventions_for_Alcohol_Dependence_i
n_Europe.pdf

[233]Answer to UK parliamentary question (2015)
http://www.parliament.uk/business/publications/written-
questions-answers-statements/written-

question/Commons/2015-01-16/221067/

[234] Alcohol Survey Reveals 'Lost Decade' Between Ages of Disorder Onset and Treatment (2007)

http://www.nih.gov/news/pr/jul2007/niaaa-02.htm

[235]Recovery From DSM–IV Alcohol Dependence United States, 2001–2002 (2006)

http://pubs.niaaa.nih.gov/publications/arh29-2/131-142.pdf

[236] Factors associated with untreated remissions from alcohol abuse or dependence (2000)
http://www.sciencedirect.com/science/article/pii/S0304460398001300#

[237] Stability of remission from alcohol dependence without formal help (2006)

http://alcalc.oxfordjournals.org/content/41/3/311

[238] Study Links Receptor to Stress-Induced Alcohol Relapse (2006)
http://www.niaaa.nih.gov/news-events/news-releases/study-links-receptor-stress-induced-alcohol-relapse

[239] Men are more likely than women to crave alcohol when they feel negative emotions (2008)
http://www.eurekalert.org/pub_releases/2008-05/ace-mam050908.php

[240240240] Rates and correlates of relapse among individuals in remission from DSM-IV alcohol dependence: a 3-year follow-up (2007)
http://www.ncbi.nlm.nih.gov/pubmed/18034696

[241] Estimating the effect of help-seeking on achieving recovery from alcohol dependence (2006)

http://www.ncbi.nlm.nih.gov/pubmed/16696626

[242] Maturing out of alcohol dependence: the impact of transitional life events

http://www.ncbi.nlm.nih.gov/pubmed/16568565

[243] Acute withdrawal, protracted abstinence and negative affect in alcoholism: Are they linked? (2010)
http://www.ncbi.nlm.nih.gov/pmc/articles/PMC3268458/

[244] Negative and Positive Alcohol Expectancies as Predictors of Abstinence after Discharge from a Residential Treatment Program: A One-Month and Three-Month Follow-up Study in Men
http://www.jsad.com/doi/pdf/10.15288/jsa.1994.55.543

[245] Distinct Effects of Protracted Withdrawal on Affect, Craving, Selective Attention and Executive Functions among Alcohol-Dependent Patients
http://alcalc.oxfordjournals.org/content/45/3/241

[246] Damaged gait and balance can recover with long-term abstinence from alcohol
http://www.eurekalert.org/pub_releases/2011-09/ace-dga090811.php

[247] Changes in the Episodic Memory and Executive Functions of Abstinent and Relapsed Alcoholics Over a 6-Month Period (2010)
http://onlinelibrary.wiley.com/doi/10.1111/j.1530-0277.2008.00859.x/abstract

[248] Cognitive remediation therapy during treatment for alcohol dependence (2012)
http://www.ncbi.nlm.nih.gov/pubmed/22630801

[249] Neuropsychological Rehabilitation in Alcohol-Related Brain Damage: A Systematic Review
http://alcalc.oxfordjournals.org/content/48/6/704.abstract

[250] Exercise may be an effective and nonpharmacologic treatment option for alcohol dependence (2010)
http://www.eurekalert.org/pub_releases/2010-06/ace-emb061410.php

[251] Transitions In and Out of Alcohol Use Disorders: Their Associations with Conditional Changes in Quality of Life Over a 3-Year Follow-Up Interval (2008)

http://www.ncbi.nlm.nih.gov/pmc/articles/PMC260552 2/#R27

252 Handbook of Clinical Neurology
http://www.elsevier.com/books/book-series/handbook-of-clinical-neurology

253 Resolution of drinking problems without formal treatment (1997)
http://onlinelibrary.wiley.com/doi/10.1111/j.1744-6163.1997.tb00544.x/abstract

254 The challenge of sobriety: Natural recovery without treatment and self-help groups (1997)

http://www.sciencedirect.com/science/article/pii/S089932 899790005

255 Alcohol Use Disorder (2013)
http://www.nytimes.com/health/guides/disease/alcoholism/medications.html

256 NPY Suppresses Stress-Induced Alcohol Relapse in Rats (2010)
http://www.niaaa.nih.gov/research/niaaa-research-highlights/npy-suppresses-stress-induced-alcohol-relapse-rats

257 Rats can't get drunk after a dose of oxytocin hormone (2015)
http://www.newscientist.com/article/dn27016-rats-cant-get-drunk-after-a-dose-of-oxytocin-hormone.html?utm_source=NSNS&utm_medium=SOC&utm_campaign=hoot&cmpid=SOC%257CNSNS%257C2014-GLOBAL-hoot#.VSPPB_msVb5

258 UCLA researchers discover how drug binds to neurons to stop drunken symptoms of alcohol (2006)
http://www.eurekalert.org/pub_releases/2006-05/uoc--urd050406.php

259 Pursuing Happiness: The Architecture of Sustainable

Change (2005)

http://sonjalyubomirsky.com/wp-content/themes/sonjalyubomirsky/papers/LSS2005.pdf
The Pursuit of Happiness: Time, Money, and Social Connection (2010)

https://www.brown.edu/academics/philosophy/ethical-inquiry/sites/brown.edu.academics.philosophy.ethical-inquiry/files/uploads/Mogilner%20Psych%20Science%202010%20Time%20Money%20and%20Social%20Connection.pdf

# Index

"alpha-delta" sleep, 122

118A, 85

118G, 85, 87, 165

abstainers, 112, 113, 141, 189, 195, 197

Acamprosate, 203

Aguadiente de Taos

Taos Lightening, 29

Alcohol Concern, 21, 194

alcohol dehydrogenase, 57

alcohol myopia, 97, 100, 102, 104, 107, 173

Alcoholics Anonymous (AA), 174

Alzheimer, 33, 60

and World Anti-Doping Agency, 75

anhedonia, 173, 199

Antisocial Personality Disorder, 191, 192

anxiety, 21, 36, 37, 42, 43, 76, 88, 90, 91, 98, 125,

127, 134, 135, 136, 138, 139, 140, 141, 148, 180, 191, 192, 197, 199, 200, 201, 205

apes, 38, 41, 87

Asian flush, 58

Asterix, 46

autonomic nervous system, 120, 137

autonomy, 15, 114, 175

Barratt Impulsivity Scale (BIS), 106

basal ganglia, 70

beer guzzling, 80

Benjamin Franklin, 204

binge drinking, 17, 43, 75, 156, 158, 159, 162, 163

Binge drinking, 37, 168

blood-brain barrier, 68

Bracknell, 45

British Pharmaceutical Industries, 30

*C elegans* roundworm, 124

calories, 30, 57

Carl Warburg, 26

Catch-22, 171

chaos theory, 188

Charenton Omnibus, 28

Chartreuse, 26

*Cheers,*, 47

children, 14, 29, 46, 47, 48, 78, 79, 82, 115, 198, 202

Christmas, 79

chronic fatigue, 120

Cleveland, 45

cocaine, 83, 167, 191, 192

cognitive depletion, 108, 109

Cognitive dysfunctions, 158

cognitive flexibility, 143

cognitive problems, 36, 148

common sense, 11, 12, 14, 16, 18, 31, 37, 155

Compatibilists, 177

*Confection Damocratric*, 27

continuum hypothesis, 156

corporate responsibility, 139

craving, 19, 147, 152, 153, 167, 206

Dale's principle, 74

*delirium tremens*, 32

denial, 112, 144, 151

dependence, 11, 17, 19, 20, 26, 32, 58, 81, 82, 86, 114, 133, 134, 135, 136, 140, 143, 146, 147, 148, 151, 152, 157, 159, 161, 163, 166, 167, 171, 173, 184, 187, 191, 193, 194, 196, 197, 198, 199, 203, 205

dependency, 10, 12, 19, 20, 51, 55, 60, 76, 88, 89, 98, 122, 127, 143, 144, 145, 148, 150, 155, 170, 190, 196, 197, 198, 200, 201, 203

depression, 21, 32, 36, 37, 43, 81, 88, 89, 92, 120, 122, 134, 135, 136, 137, 138, 139, 140, 141, 157, 191, 192, 205

Diagnostic and Statistical Manual of Mental Disorders, 145

Disulfiram, 203

DIY approach

to abstaining, 196

Dogs, 64

dopamine, 58, 76, 85, 87, 88, 92, 93, 94, 95, 164, 186

Douglas Fairbanks, 55

Dr Pierre Ordinaire, 28

Drink Aware, 138, 157

Drink Responsibly, 139

Dutch courage, 44, 90, 100

*Eastenders*, 47

Education, 18

encephalisation quotient, 64

Epicurus, 204

Ernest Hemingway, 208

expectancies, 39, 41, 49, 50, 54, 139

expectations, 14, 39, 41, 42, 43, 44, 45, 46, 48, 49, 50, 51, 52, 53, 55, 98, 108

Facebook, 109, 111, 113, 168, 207

fibromyalgia, 120

films, 47

Finnish identical twins, 89

France, 28, 34, 43

Franklin, 206

free will, 13, 50, 62, 170, 172, 174, 175, 176, 184

GABA, 74, 76, 94

Galen, 61

Gallic approach, 79

gamma-aminobutyric acid (GABA), 74

genetics, 57, 124, 131

George Jean Nathan, 97

glial cells, 70

glutamate receptor, 82

Google+, 207

Gothenburg, 195

grand wormwood, 28

gravitation, 10

grey matter, 68, 69

guideline maximum, 13, 20, 190

Guinness, 31

gun industry, 16

hangover, 26, 60, 75, 76, 89, 119, 123, 124, 125, 126, 127, 128, 129, 130, 131, 132, 133, 147, 148, 159, 182, 208

happiness, 13, 15, 17, 20, 21, 89, 187, 204, 205, 206, 209, 210

hard determinists, 176, 177

Harry Houdini, 55

Hawkeye Pierce, 46, 208

higher power, 174

Hippocrates, 24, 61

home comfort, 23, 31

hummingbirds, 64

Humphrey Bogart, 46

Hunter Thompson, 208

hypervigilance, 54

hypothalamus, 68, 94

Iago, 16, 212

immune system, 122, 133

Impulse, 105

impulse control, 143

impulsivity, 96, 104, 105, 106, 108, 109, 158, 161, 203

Inebriation, 97, 103, 181, 208

Infant rats, 78

International Statistical Classification of Diseases (ICD), 146

Italy, 35, 43, 194

James Bond, 17, 208

Jefferson Airplane, 83

jellyfish, 63

Jeremy Clarkson, 178

Jerry Leadbetter, 47

Keith Richards, 208

Kit Carson, 29

kola nut, 31

Labiton, 30

Lady Nancy Astor, 210

Libertarians, 177

LinkedIn, 207

liverish, 56

lost decade, 193

M*A*S*H, 46, 208

Mahatma Gandhi, 55

major depression, 136, 140

marijuana, 191, 192

Marvin Minsky, 67

Mediterranean diet, 35

Mental Health Foundation, 42

methyl alcohol, 33

mood and anxiety disorders (MADs), 140

moral fibre, 95

Morse, 46

Mr Magoo, 97, 100

mu-opioid receptor variant, 84

Naltrexone, 202

Nancy Reagan, 50

National Collegiate Athletic Association, 75

Netherlands, 43

neuron, 70, 71, 72, 73, 74, 76, 156, 165

Neuropeptide Y, 203

neurotransmitter, 58, 74, 75, 76, 85, 86, 92, 93, 165

never-again-syndrome, 110

Norm, 47, 208

Norway, 43

Ontario, 195, 196

opiates, 192

Oxytocin, 203

p mice, 81

Paracelsus, 25

placebo, 15, 52, 53, 54, 98, 107, 129

politics, 114

polyphenols, 34

positron emission tomography (PET), 85

Prince Albert, 24

prohibition, 114, 206

psychedelic drugs, 60

psychiatric department admissions, 32

quantum mechanics, 10

Queen Victoria, 24, 25

racing drivers, 16

rapid eye movement (REM), 118

rat, 39, 66, 80, 84, 94, 95, 208

REM, 118, 119, 122, 200

René Descartes, 61

rheumatoid arthritis, 120

*Rhubarb*, 27

Richard Feynman, 55

Romania, 43

Royal Society of Medicine, 29

salience, 92, 93

sea squirts, 63

Seizures, 199

self-control, 108, 109

serotonin transporter gene, 86

sexual dysfunction, 19, 137

Shakespeare, 16, 171

sherry, 31

sleep, 21, 24, 31, 59, 60, 69, 74, 77, 86, 88, 116, 117, 118, 119, 120, 121, 122, 126, 129, 131, 199, 200, 202

smokers, 98, 147, 192

smug, 111, 112, 113

South Dakota, 48

sponges, 63

starfish, 63

Stephen King, 55

Stroop Task, 129

Synapse, 72, 73

tail brain, 63

teeneagers, 79

thalamus, 68

the Alcohol Hangover Research Group, 125

the British Pharmacopoeia, 30

*The Good Life*, 47

*The Independent*, 111

*The Society of Mind*, 67

the wagon, 113

the World Health Organisation, 190

Theodore Roosevelt, 55

Theophrastus Bombastus von Hohenheim, 25

Thomas Jefferson, 206

*Top Gear*, 178

trust, 88, 182, 201

Turkey, 43

Twitter, 168, 207

UK, 18, 21, 42, 43, 47, 71, 72, 104, 138, 154, 155, 157, 159, 162, 188, 189, 194

UNESCO, 34

US, 16, 21, 29, 32, 47, 48, 50, 80, 105, 134, 145, 146, 147, 163, 179, 180, 189, 191, 192, 193, 198, 202, 206, 208

*veisalgia*, 123

vigilance tasks, 158

Warburg's Tincture, 26

whisky, 16, 31, 37, 45

white matter, 68, 71

White Rabbit, 83

William White, 29

Winston Churchill, 208

Wisconsin Card Sorting Task, 166

withdrawal, 23, 26, 27, 32, 60, 81, 89, 126, 127, 133, 144, 145, 146, 147, 148, 152, 153, 171, 188, 198, 205, 209

women, 11, 18, 49, 57, 104, 107, 119, 130, 158, 163, 180, 189, 191, 193, 195, 199

*Zedoary root*, 27

■

Printed in Great Britain
by Amazon